WHAT AMERICANS SHOULD DO ABOUT CRIME

What Americans Should Do about Crime

L. HAROLD DeWOLF

Drawings by FRANCES P. MITCHELL

HARPER & ROW, PUBLISHERS

NEW YORK, HAGERSTOWN

SAN FRANCISCO, LONDON

Designed by Sidney Feinberg

Library of Congress Cataloging in Publication Data

De Wolf, Iotan Harold, 1905–
    What Americans should do about crime.
    Includes bibliographical references.
    1. Criminal justice, Administration of—United
States.   2. Crime and criminals—United States.
I. Title.
HV8138.D43   1976   364'.973   75–36728
ISBN 0–06–061912–0 pbk.

---

76 77 78 79 10 9 8 7 6 5 4 3 2

What Americans Should Do About Crime is a condensed version of the main facts and ideas reported and documented in the author's larger book *Crime and Justice in America: A Paradox of Conscience*, published by Harper & Row in 1975. The research and the writing of both books were assisted by an expense grant from the National Endowment for the Humanities. These books do not necessarily represent views of the Endowment.

CONTENTS

Part V. How Americans Should Deal With Crime

WHAT AMERICANS SHOULD DO ABOUT CRIME

PART I

THE PLAGUE OF CRIME

■

1. Present Volume and Kinds of Crime

"Serious Crime Up 16 Percent in '74; Trend Continues"
"Shop Owner Shot Dead in Robbery"
"Grandmother Raped in Her Home"
"Teenager and Policeman Killed in Shootout At Suspected Drug Center"

So we read in the headlines. Where will it all end? What can we do about the appalling crimes which have engulfed the United States and seem always on the rise? Why can't the police protect us any more? Are corrupt politicians to blame? Or soft sentences from permissive judges? Where does the home fit in the picture? Is there something more the church should be doing? The school? You and I? What should Americans be doing?

If we are to find useful answers we need to begin by getting our facts straight, for there are many airy theories and myths in circulation which are based on misinformation. They divert attention away from important parts of the problem and discourage the more promising efforts.

Myths and Realities.

1. *Myth:* The Federal Bureau of Investigation keeps records and reports regularly on the kinds of crime, called Index crimes, which take most life and property.

1

Reality: The FBI does regularly report figures on seven kinds of crime—criminal homicide, forcible rape, robbery, aggravated assault, burglary, automobile theft, and larceny-theft. The news stories under such headlines as the first one above usually cover these Uniform Crime Reports by the FBI. But the one crime of drunken driving kills more people than all Index crimes combined, while fraud and embezzlement take more property than all the Index crimes. Yet the FBI does not include drunken driving nor fraud nor embezzlement in its periodic reports on trends in serious crime.

2. *Myth:* The Uniform Crime Report figures on the seven Index crimes, issued periodically by the FBI, are reasonably accurate.

Reality: Only the figures on homicides are reasonably accurate. On the average the police report to the FBI only about half of the Index crimes on which they have received word. The proportion they report fluctuates widely, in response to political pressures. If the mayor or chief of police has promised to reduce crime, police officers know he would like to show a decrease and they become more lax about filling out the UCR forms. Recently the Law Enforcement Assistance Administration reported that in Philadelphia there were over five Index crimes committed to every one recorded for the FBI. On the other hand, if a police department is making a major effort to secure more funds, a crime wave may appear on paper because of pressure on every officer to be especially diligent in recording on the forms every crime reported to him. Perhaps the pressures tend to even out nationally, but for local comparisons the figures must be viewed with considerable skepticism.*

3. *Myth:* Most serious crimes are reported to the police.

Reality: About half of Index-type crimes are reported to the police. Only homicides and motor vehicle thefts are reported fairly reliably. "Murder will out," and owners of stolen cars want to collect their insurance.

4. *Myth:* Most arrests the police make are for Index crimes.

Reality: Police make more arrests for public drunkenness (not drunken driving) alone than for all Index crimes combined. Index crimes account for a small proportion of arrests.

5. *Myth:* When people who commit crime are not convicted and punished, that is usually due to failure of the courts.

Reality: In connection with most serious crimes no one is arrested. Of Index crimes committed, about 50% are reported to the police. In about 26% of cases reported, or 13% of cases of crime

---

* Statistical and other factual statements are documented in the author's larger book *Crime and Justice in America: A Paradox of Conscience,* recently published by Harper & Row.

committed, the police make arrests of suspects. Of the original 100 serious crimes (felonies) committed, 5 result in juveniles being bound over to juvenile court, 3.2 in felony charges and 2.9 in felony convictions. If persons arrested represent a fair sample of the ratio between juveniles and adults actually committing felonious acts, then of crimes committed by adults, 5¼% result in felony charges and 4.7% in felony convictions. Of those charged nearly 90% result in findings of guilty and in consequent sentencing. (Clarence Schrag gives the basic figures in a study for the National Institute of Mental Health Center for Studies of Crime, 1965.) Lest you put too much blame on the police, you should remember that half the crimes are never brought to their attention and you should note also that in many other cases no citizens can be found who are able and willing to testify.

6. *Myth:* One reason we have so much crime is that American judges impose softer sentences than judges in other developed countries.

Reality: For Index-type crimes harsher sentences are imposed and longer prison terms are actually served than in any other developed country. For example, in Holland or Norway prison terms for similar crimes range generally from one-third to one-fifth as long as in the United States. Some countries do impose more severe sentences for drunken driving. For example, judges in Norway and Sweden almost invariably impose short jail sentences in addition to suspending licenses.

7. *Myth:* Use of the death penalty would reduce crime or at least murders.

Reality: In many studies, similar neighboring states, one with and one without the death penalty, have been compared, as have single states during periods with and without it. Similar comparisons have been made among nations, of which many ceased to use capital punishment long ago. In none of these comparisons has the death penalty appeared to reduce the number of murders. In fact the very slight differences observed show more murders where the death penalty is in use. A study commission of the California legislature found that in years when there were executions in both California and Pennsylvania murders in those states increased about 25% on days near the dates of executions, an increase for which no other explanation could be found.

8. *Myth:* Most inmates in our prisons were convicted by judges or juries.

Reality: Most inmates—about 90%—pleaded guilty, most of them by plea bargaining: that is, a deal was negotiated by prosecuting and defense attorneys, by which the defendant pleaded guilty to a lesser offense than that charged, or even to the very offense charged, but in return for a promise by the prosecutor to recommend a lighter sentence than the usual one for the offense named in the indictment. Sometimes the judge was a party to the agreement. The defendant then went to court only for accepting of the plea by a judge and the pronouncing of sentence.

9. *Myth:* Since the Supreme Court has required that legal counsel be provided for all defendants in criminal cases, rich and poor now have fairly equal justice in the courts.

Reality: Affluent defendants usually have more and better service from their personally retained attorneys, as well as bail money to let them out to prepare their cases. With these advantages and also more sympathetic understanding of judges and juries, they are less likely to be convicted of serious charges and when convicted are almost sure to receive more lenient treatment.

10. *Myth:* If a judge imposes a sentence which, under all the circumstances, seems unfair, a defense lawyer can appeal the case.

Reality: In most states, while a conviction can be appealed, a sentence, even if outrageous, cannot be appealed unless the judge violated a law in imposing it.

11. *Myth:* Attempts are made to rehabilitate most inmates of our prisons.

Reality: Programs of rehabilitation, such as therapy, education, and vocational training, touch only a small percentage of inmates. Most prisoners are simply stored away in cages, largely in enforced idleness.

12. *Myth:* Rehabilitation is a failure anyway. Former Attorney General Saxbe said rehabilitation was a myth and he bemoaned the millions of dollars wasted on it. Once a criminal always a criminal.

Reality: While most official programs of rehabilitation prove disappointing, the majority of offenders do, with the help of various influences, rehabilitate themselves. Two-thirds of the persons convicted of serious crimes are never convicted a second time. But some offenders are convicted of several or many crimes in a period of years. As a result, about two-thirds of convictions are of repeaters. Even of these recidivists many eventually stop their criminal activities. In fact most criminals quit crime in their forties if not earlier.

13. *Myth:* Prison sentences have been extensively used as punishment for crime for many centuries and all round the world.

Reality: The practice of measuring out prison sentences as punishment for crime is an American invention. It began in Philadelphia in 1790 and rapidly spread over the world. It is true that debtors' prisons had long been used in some countries, but these were devices, mostly unsuccessful, for collecting debts, not measured punishments for crime. From much earlier times imprisonment has been used to detain people awaiting trial or executive decision, as in the case of the Apostle Paul in Rome, or to prevent rivals from leading revolts against a king. Punishments for crime have been of many kinds, from execution with torture to public exposure in stocks, ducking, required restitution to victims, and monetary fines.

14. *Myth:* Most people who commit felonies are mentally ill.

Reality: By no norm of psychiatric practice are most of them mentally ill.

15. *Myth:* Behavior modification, B. F. Skinner–style, has the answer to problems of rehabilitation.

Reality: Attempts to rehabilitate by short-term incentive and artificial conditioning, without regard to personal problems, ideals and goals, have produced only short-term results. Behavior modification has been well tried at the federal Robert F. Kennedy Youth Center in West Virginia. It has been given up as a failure for purposes of lasting rehabilitation.

16. *Myth:* Most violent crime is the work of a national or international organized syndicate.

Reality: There are many organized groups which operate rackets and corrupt both business and politics. But they are ever-changing, and mostly local, although many are loosely related in regional groups or a national syndicate. Most murders are provoked by special situations and few people who kill ever do it a second time.

17. *Myth:* Because most criminals have serious emotional or characterological problems, only skilled professionals have much chance of helping them go straight.

Reality: Volunteers, of whom there are now many thousands, working with courts and probation officers after reasonably careful screening, with a little training and great personal concern, are superior in achievement to most professional workers in official programs without aid from volunteer citizens.

Further Facts About Crime.

In amount of violent crime, the United States stands alone among developed countries of the West. The comparative figures on criminal homicides are fairly reliable. According to such figures, as compiled by the Metropolitan Life Insurance Company, white males in the United States, per 100,000, commit three times as many criminal homicides as males of all races in Canada, seven times as many as males of France, eight times as many as males in the United Kingdom or Japan, and ten times as many as those of Scandinavia and the Netherlands. Non-white males in this country commit approximately ten times as many per 100,000 as do white males.

In all developed countries, violent crimes and also such crimes as burglary and larceny-theft are most numerous among the poorest people and among minorities who feel deprived and shut out from full participation in the privileges and power of the majority.

However, more people are killed and more property is taken in the United States by crime of kinds more heavily represented among the middle and upper economic classes. Safety experts generally estimate that about half the motor vehicle deaths and injuries involve intoxicated drivers. This means that about 28,000 persons per year are killed by intoxicated drivers, as compared to about 19,000 victims of criminal homicide. In property crimes, the FBI released an unusual one-time report of another agency, showing that in the fiscal year 1974 banks and savings and loan associations lost more than five and one-half times as much by embezzlement and fraud as by robbery.

In 1960 the Justice Department exposed a criminal conspiracy of the largest electrical manufacturers in the United States. Seven highly placed executives served short prison terms for their illegal activities which had cost the American people many millions of dollars. In fact, about 60% of the largest corporations have been convicted in the courts of criminal business practices, but usually their executives have not been sent to prison.

Watergate, the exposure of former Vice President Spiro Agnew's criminal dishonesty, and other criminal abuses of power by members of the Richard M. Nixon Administration revealed the presence of crime at the very top in American politics.

Although the kinds of crime vary with the position of offenders as inside or outside the structures of power and wealth, crime is a scandalous monster from top to bottom of present American life.

What should we do about it? This is an ethical question as are all issues concerning human decisions.

2. Possible Responses

Vindictive Anger Against the Few Caught and Convicted.

When you hear or read in the news about an especially cruel or destructive crime in your community, what is your emotional response to it? If it is a combination of fear and anger you are probably a typical citizen. The general response is similar when headlines announce another increase in the numbers of robberies, rapes, murders, and violent assaults.

The fear leads many Americans to hide indoors at night or to avoid going out alone in an inner city. But this does not solve the problem. Some people must go out by necessity and the streets are more dangerous because so few pedestrians are on them. Besides, crimes invade our homes and business establishments. What ought we to do to reduce crime? When this question is asked, most people respond in anger.

They demand that the police "crack down on crime." They call for the death penalty for a lengthening list of crimes and longer prison sentences for others. We may inwardly cheer when the police or private citizens shoot and kill suspected burglars, rapists, or purse snatchers—unless something about the incident makes us fear that the gun of a trigger-happy person might be turned against us or our friends by mistake.

Our vindictive anger against the criminal offenders is largely frustrated by the escape of most people who have committed criminal acts. When less than one-eighth of them are caught and far fewer can be successfully prosecuted, we are left to vent our anger against those few, and we do, with the longest prison terms

anywhere among the developed nations of the free world and, until recently, the most use of the death penalty.

Has it worked? The rising rates of crime in the states using the harshest punishments, as well as in others, indicate that it does not.

Is it right? Is public vengeance against the many criminals, in high places and low, properly taken out on the small sample arrested, prosecuted and convicted?

Is vindictive retribution the proper purpose of criminal justice? What is justice when a crime has been committed?

These questions will be given much further attention. But we must note that some official commissions and many persons seriously studying the problem advocate other responses.

Attacking Causes of Crime.

The President's Commission on Law Enforcement and Administration of Justice which reported in 1967 made many recommendations affecting the system of criminal justice. But the commission reported also that crime would continue in heavy volume until the basic social causes of crime were changed. Such causes included crowding in the cities, extremes of wealth and serious poverty side by side, excessively zealous pursuit of the dollar, and disorganized family life, among others.

In 1971 the Law Enforcement Assistance Administration of the Justice Department established the National Advisory Commission on Criminal Justice Standards and Goals. When the Advisory Commission reported in 1973, one of its five big volumes was on *Community Crime Prevention*. That volume includes "recommendations for increasing the educational level of youth, for increasing job opportunities and skills, and for increasing recreational opportunities" (p. 3), along with other preventive activities.

Other needed attacks on causes of crime include making medical care available to all, prevention and treatment of drug and alcohol addiction and a consistent system of sustaining support for the poor in place of the present patchwork of welfare measures which leave out many of the most deserving workers and their families, while duplicating aid to others. Television needs to reduce stress on violence and on competitive acquiring of material things.

Reorganizing Criminal Justice.

All these attacks on the causes of crime make some new demands on the system of criminal justice. Besides, there are more than one million people caught up in the system at any given time. Some are under arrest or awaiting trial. Others are on probation, in jail, in prison, in halfway houses or on parole. Juveniles are awaiting trial or are under sentence or prescribed treatment as delinquents. As the system is now operating, hundreds of thousands of these persons will be committing further crimes. More than three million Americans go to jail or to prison each year.

There is a much larger number who have committed crimes but have not been caught and prosecuted.

Hence, whatever else is done, we need urgently to see how the criminal justice system itself can be reorganized to be more effective. This system has only part of the responsibility for reducing crime, true. But it does have an important part and it is not doing it well.

In this book we shall be mainly concerned with the ways we deal with crime actually committed and ways we ought to deal with it. At the same time, we shall be aware that other policies concerning health, education, recreation, and economic justice are essential in a national program of crime reduction.

QUESTIONS FOR THOUGHT

1. Have you been a victim of theft, burglary, robbery, violent assault, forcible rape, or the stealing of a motor vehicle in the last five years? If so, did you report it to the police? Why did you or did you not report it?
2. In the same period of five years, have you been a victim of fraudulent merchandising, a bad check, or other white-collar crime?
3. Do the police in your community report to the FBI all crimes reported to them? Do the Uniform Crime Reports fairly represent crimes actually committed in your community?
4. What are the crimes for which most arrests are made in your community?
5. Why do you think the Uniform Crime Reports of Index crimes do not include the crimes which kill the most people or those which take the most property?
6. Have you ever observed proceedings in a criminal court?
7. In what ways does crime injure the interests of other people besides persons attacked and innocent buyers of stolen property?
8. Has your community a healthy wholeness which gives all groups a sense of pride in it and a stake in defending its order?
9. What could your church or other organization do to help lower the crime rate?
10. Does the handling of juvenile delinquents in your city or county help to prepare them for law-abiding lives?
11. What do you think should be the purpose of criminal justice?

SUGGESTED FURTHER READING

RAMSEY CLARK, *Crime in America*. Paperback. New York: Pocket Books, 1970.

Information Please Almanac or *World Almanac* of the current year:
Paperbacks in which you will find many of the latest statistics
on crime and justice as well as a wide variety of other
information.

PHILIP WOGAMAN, *Guaranteed Annual Income: The Moral Issues.*
Paperback. Nashville: Abingdon Press, 1968.

PART II

CRIMINAL JUSTICE IN TROUBLE

■

3. Public Disrepute

People express in many ways their low opinion of the law and its enforcement. One way is to commit great numbers of crimes. This expression is occurring in all classes of society and with a vengeance. But a low opinion is being registered also in other ways.

Lack of Public Cooperation.

When only about half of the victims of crime report to the police we must ask why. Do they not care that the criminals are escaping scot-free to injure other people? The question has been systematically studied and various answers have been given.

Some victims say they are afraid of reprisals if they talk. Others say it would do no good because the police could not or would not catch the offenders anyway and even if they did the courts would not punish them. Many victims say they have had enough trouble from the crime itself without now putting themselves through hours of grilling by the police, losing days of work to await being called to testify in court and suffering the further indignities of cross-examination when they do take the stand.

A few victims think the law is vengeful and unjust, doing no

15

one any good and making more bitter and violent the people it puts in jail or prison.

Notice that all these reasons have in common a low regard for the law and its agencies of enforcement.

Even when victims complain, the police can seldom arrest the culprits without more information than the victims alone can give. After the police make arrests, police and prosecutors cannot usually file criminal charges without witnesses. In most cases witnesses able and willing to testify are hard to find.

You have probably read of some violent crimes committed in plain view of a dozen or more people, none of whom lifted a hand to rescue the victim or even left the window from which they were watching to call the police on the telephone. Their common theme song was "I did not want to get involved." But why?

Again many reasons are given. But one common component is a negative attitude toward the police and other agencies of the criminal justice system. Most people want to leave the whole problem of crime to the professionals, mainly the police, and blame them for the prevalence of crime. The same people have a low opinion of these guardians of the law and refuse to cooperate with them. This lack of cooperation makes their work difficult and in many cases impossible.

Special Hostility of Some Important Classes.

The police are the visible presence of the law best known to civilians. Public attitudes toward the police are therefore especially important signs of attitudes toward the system of criminal justice. The signs are disturbingly low in those segments of the population most critically important for law enforcement.

Two classes of people are conspicuous for their large proportions of felonious offenders. The non-white residents of neglected, poverty-stricken centers of our inner cities include disproportionate numbers both of victims and of people committing Index crimes. Most persons who commit such crimes anywhere are young. It is precisely among non-white people in the cities and young people generally that opinions of the police are most unfavorable.

According to the FBI, nearly half of all arrests for Index crimes in 1973 were of youth seventeen or younger. Violent crimes hit their peak at age eighteen and property crimes at age sixteen. To say that the police are not well liked by the young is an understatement. Teenagers and young people through the college years tend to dislike authority figures generally. But since the 1960s a special hostility has been focused on the police. It was fomented in many confrontations between antiwar demonstrators and civil rights activists, on the one hand, and police on the other. The overt expressions of such feelings were muted by 1975, but much bad feeling persists, both among college youth and among young people of similar age not in college.

Male youth in the later teens frequently complain that the police pull them off the road and give them speeding tickets when older drivers going faster are ignored. Young people describe police as contemptuous or hostile toward them at night and in other ways discriminating against them.

The police tell a different story about youth, giving accounts of harassment, drug traffic, vandalism, dangerous driving, and public disorder. They have the figures of automobile insurance companies to support their reports, at least of the dangerous driving.

The bad feeling between youth and the police begins early. A study in Cincinnati found that in the junior high schools a majority of white boys said the police accuse boys of things they did not do. A larger majority of black boys thought the police were mean. Reports from other cities gave similar results. In the inner cities great numbers of boys look on the police as "the enemy." When we remember that careers of violent crime most often begin in the junior high school years, we see the importance of such attitudes.

Among black adults in the cities the low opinion of police takes a different form, but it is pervasive. They complain most frequently that the police provide little protection in their neighborhoods. This belief leads to even poorer reporting and cooperation than are present elsewhere and also to larger proportions of households being armed for their own self-defense. Many guns bought for such self-defense are later stolen by criminals or are used by the buyers in quarrels or against innocent neighbors mistaken for intruders—with tragic results.

When people are hostile to the law as embodied by the police, lawless acts are numerous.

Why the Disrepute?

Why do so many people throughout our society, and especially among the youth and the minorities, have such low opinions of the law and its enforcement? It is important to know the causes of beliefs that our system of criminal justice is unjust or inept. So long as such beliefs are prevalent as they are now, unscrupulous citizens will take advantage of the law's unpopularity by criminal acts against others and even law-abiding citizens will continue to give poor cooperation to agencies of law enforcement.

We can discount at once some of the disrepute in which many citizens hold the law. Those who want to steal, defraud, or otherwise prey upon their neighbors will be sure to despise the law which stands in their way. Other citizens may subconsciously lean to a similar low opinion of police, courts, and corrections because it gives them an excuse to avoid inconvenient cooperation. If I am convinced that the police won't do anything anyway, or that even if they do, the courts will turn the criminals loose, then I do not feel obliged to report as a victim or witness of crime. I may feel similarly relieved from involvement if I decide that the police and courts are unjust and corrections incapable of doing any good.

But such escapist attitudes in a democratic society mark a road to ever-increasing, disastrous crime and eventual anarchy. If we are to live as free citizens in an orderly society, we must examine the grounds for charges against the system and seek to eradicate them. When citizens refuse to be involved in efforts to defend and increase justice, they are choosing a well-worn road through crime and anarchy to tyranny.

In actuality, the system of criminal justice as it now operates in the United States deserves many of the criticisms it receives. When we examine it closely, we shall find it riddled with injustice and inexcusably wasteful of both material resources and people. We shall see that underlying its injustice and wastefulness are a pervasive confusion of purpose at every level and basic conflict of aims among its different agencies.

4. Injustice

Unjust Police Action and Prosecution.

The task of a police officer, especially in a large urban department is both difficult and confusing. He finds himself in a conflict of roles and it is hard for him to know what is expected of him.

The average police person spends most of the time on the job maintaining order and helping citizens in trouble, not hunting down and arresting criminals. A common day's work includes such activities as helping to find a lost child, making sure that shop doors are locked after hours, warning children against disturbing or dangerous activities, assisting people taken ill on the street, and quieting down a domestic quarrel.

On the other hand, the dominant understanding in urban police departments is that if an officer is to impress his superiors and get regular promotions, he needs to earn a reputation as an "aggressive cop" who makes a large number of arrests. To accomplish this, he stops people on slight grounds of suspicion or for petty infractions ordinarily overlooked, questions them, and hopes that among the many he stops some will prove subject to arrest for serious offenses. Some people he stops may be angered by his aggressiveness and respond in ways which provide ground for arrest. The patrolman who prefers to give friendly warning and counsel to the gang of youth on the street corner, rather than building an arrest record, may turn many boys away from delinquency and crime, but he usually gets little credit for it from his superiors.

On the other hand, if an aggressive police officer is rough and discourteous toward the wrong people, such as prominent business persons and potentially influential people, this may get him into trouble with his superiors.

What, then, is the ambitious police officer to do? The answer is easy. Be the helping gentleman or lady to the more settled and affluent citizen, but assume the suspicious and aggressive role to confront the less stable, youthful, rootless, and poor people. Members of groups known to be unpopular with the dominant po-

litical and economic powers in the community are especially likely to be regarded as fair game for harassment. Young people with completely clean records as drivers have found that by putting on their automobile bumpers the insignia of organizations known to be disliked, they would quickly develop records for traffic offenses.

Many persons going into police work are fine, public-spirited young people. But many others are attracted by the role of aggressive power to be exercised over other people. The immunities which police uniforms usually bestow on rough behavior and the rewards which often follow tend to increase these emotional inclinations.

An important problem of police conduct concerns relations with people having records of arrest. When a crime is under investigation, the first thought of the police is usually of people in the vicinity who have served sentences for crime. Even if a man formerly arrested has been found not guilty, the police are likely to take a dim view of that finding. Hence they feel free to stop and question on sight anyone with an arrest record. They presume that even if he is not guilty of the crime being investigated he is probably engaged in some other illegal activity. From the police point of view, a person with a record of previous arrest is likely to be presumed guilty until he can prove his innocence.

Many men complain that when they have returned home on parole or on completion of sentence, or even after being charged and found not guilty, they find it almost impossible to take up the normal life of a law-abiding citizen because of harassment by the police. When the police accost them in the presence of decent people with whom they now have social or business relationships and remind them of their records, the results may be so maddening that they soon return to crime.

Many young adults remember bitterly the overreaction of Chicago police against crowds of demonstrators near the Democratic convention in 1968. With deeper anguish and hostility others relive the violent and murderous assaults at Jackson State University or Kent State University. The courts have repeatedly rebuked the police and even awarded millions of dollars in damages to the thousands of citizens who were indiscriminately swept off the streets of Washington, D.C., and pushed into confinement, on May Day, 1971, because a few had boasted that they would use the demonstrations against the Vietnam War to disrupt the traffic and normal business of the capital city. In April 1973, gangs of armed men dressed as hippies but later identified as federal narcotics agents were reported to have broken into widely separated homes in Collinsville, Illinois, and terrorized the residents. In one home the man and his wife said the agents roughly bound them, ransacked the house, smashed the television set and left the house a shambles. The residents said the men refused to show identification, did not even mention a search warrant and made no apology when they confessed that they had "made a mistake" and gruffly left. In my files are authenticated reports of many other outrageous violations of law and elementary human rights by agents of law enforcement. In my hearing a highly placed police officer in Maryland boasted that under his command deadly police use of firearms had "saved the courts a lot of trouble." When a woman asked him whether they could do this under the law, he replied, "Madam, you don't seem to understand; we *are* the law." Such police assumption of duties as arresting officers, prosecutors, judges, and executioners, is fortunately unusual these days. But it is a reminder of need for public vigilance. It is also one reason for widespread low opinion of the law.

Both local police and the federal investigative agencies are frequently found to have invaded privacy by illegal eavesdropping. Samuel Dash, aided by Richard F. Schwarz and Robert E. Knowlton, made a wide study of wiretapping and other methods of intercepting messages and listening to conversations in presumed privacy. In *The Eavesdroppers* (1959) they reported that they found much of this going on in all the cities studied, despite laws strictly forbidding it in some of them. In fact, even where the law provided generously for legal methods of doing it, many policemen did not bother to ask for the legal permits. The researchers found also that many of the wiretaps were used by the police, not to fight crime, but in order to obtain payoffs by blackmail, mostly of gambling interests. The Watergate and related scandals, together with later investigations of the Federal Bureau of Investigation and the Central Intelligence Agency have brought to the surface more of such activity, much of it for personally selfish political purposes.

When people appointed or elected as guardians of justice, even at high levels of government, perpetrate upon other citizens such rank injustices and violations of criminal law, we are in deep trouble, indeed.

Injustice in the Laws.

We should expect to see some variations in the statutes of different states, cities, and rural counties in a federal union as large and varied as the United States. But there are reasonable limits. We need not have a precise definition of justice at hand to know that some differences are unjust.

Forty-seven states were reported in 1971 to have criminal laws forbidding sodomy or any kind of "unnatural" (usually undefined) sexual relations, in forty-five of those states not excepting private relations between husband and wife. Often the penalties were severe. On the other hand, Connecticut, Kansas, and Minnesota did not forbid sodomy. In the city of Dallas alone, between 1963 and July 1969, there were 451 arrests for sodomy, a non-offense in Kansas.

When a man takes advantage of a young girl's immaturity to have a sexual relation with her, even with her consent, all fifty states treat this as a serious criminal offense, under the name of statutory rape or carnal knowledge. But how young must a girl be to be thus protected by law?

If she is *ten* years old, she is on her own responsibility in Florida, South Dakota, and New Mexico. No regional matter, this! On the other hand, woe to the young man who falls for the allurements of a young woman *twenty* years of age in Tennessee! For even if she actively seeks intercourse under the age of *twenty-one* in that state, the man who unites with her commits statutory rape. The decisive age is *eighteen* in New York and many other states. There are other variations.

A homosexual act between consenting adults is not prohibited in Illinois, is a misdemeanor in New York, and is punishable by life imprisonment in some states.

A person possessing a small amount of marijuana in some jurisdictions is not even subject to arrest. On the other hand, a committee of the Texas Senate reported that in 1972, under Texas law, six first offenders convicted of simple possession were serving terms of thirty years or more, three of them sentenced for life. In California, the maximum penalty for voluntary manslaughter is ten years, but for a second offense of simple possession of marijuana the maximum was, at the same time, twenty years! Not only was recent California law on possession absurdly out of line with that of most states, but appears incredibly vindictive when compared with the penalty for intentionally killing a person without proven personal malice.

On the other hand, the use of beverage alcohol, demonstrated to be much more addictive, dangerous, and in itself productive of crime, is generally legal and socially acceptable.

The Texas Senate Drug Committee which reported on that state's indefensible drug laws in 1972 led to corrective legislation in 1973 and California reduced penalties for possession of marijuana in 1975. However, the same irrational and vindictive spirit which produced the old laws is still at work in the writing of bills before Congress and many state legislatures.

In Nebraska, a woman can incur for prostitution a penalty of not less than one year nor more than ten. Her boss, for operating a house of prostitution, faces a minimum of a $200 fine or three months, and a maximum of $1,000 or six months. In Hawaii, the prostitute would face a maximum of thirty days, while the operator of the house could get a maximum of ten years.

One kind of law which actually forces judges and juries to make unjust decisions is the law prescribing a specific mandatory sentence for a kind of crime or for repeated convictions of crime.

By prohibiting any adaptation of sentence to the circumstances of the crime, such a law pushes the judge or jury into an all-or-nothing decision. The result is that many persons are found innocent who appear to be guilty but to a degree much less than would warrant so severe a sentence. Other defendants are found guilty, and although the judge and jury regard the mandatory sentence prescribed as excessive in these cases, the judge has no alternative. For example, when the death sentence is mandatory for the crime of killing an arresting police officer, two defendants may be charged under similar circumstances. In both cases evidence may show that the officer used excessive force and otherwise goaded the defendant into violent action. There may also be some doubt whether the defendant intended to kill the officer or only, in anger, to injure him. Of the two juries, one may reluctantly decide that the defendant did indeed kill the officer and must, therefore, be found guilty. The other jury, though recognizing overwhelming evidence that the defendant did kill the officer, believes that under the circumstances the death penalty is so much too severe that justice would be better served by a verdict of innocent. In each of the two cases injustice is done and the law made impossible any more just alternative. Where heavy mandatory sentences are prescribed by law, a few people are disproportionately punished, while others, little or no less guilty are released scot-free.

Mandatory laws concerning recidivists are especially bad in this respect. When the law, for example, requires that on a third conviction—whatever the crime—a person must be sentenced for life, prosecutors usually do not tell the court that the defendant has two previous convictions, for fear the heavy penalty will prevent conviction altogether at this time, particularly if the latest offense is a mild one, perhaps a misdemeanor such as petty larceny, disorderly conduct, or public drunkenness. A study of the West Virginia law, in 1956, showed that of 904 recidivists charged with new crimes, only 79 were prosecuted as recidivists. This could mean that a prosecutor's discretion made the difference between one person receiving life imprisonment and another committing the same offense, with the same previous record, having only to pay a fine or go on probation. When the law dictates the sentence, the result will frequently be unjust.

Injustice in the Courts.

Most laws are so written as to allow the judge to choose a sentence between fairly wide limits. The judge is thus permitted to consider extenuating or aggravating circumstances, the sentence best calculated to return the convicted person to society as a law-abiding citizen, and any other factors which seem relevant and proper. Well and good. But this places a heavy responsibility on the judge. Unfortunately, individual differences among judges sometimes affect results more than the differences among the persons they sentence.

Differences among judges were put to a test in Washington, D.C., on January 26, 1973. In a make-believe but realistic court case, forty-three District of Columbia judges heard the same "evidence," then handed down "sentences" which they thought appropriate. The "sentences" ranged all the way from probation to twenty years in prison. The defendant so variably judged was fictional. But there are similar disparities of sentencing in parallel real cases tried by different judges.

Consider the fate of men who evaded or refused drafting into the military forces during the Vietnam War and who were tried while American ground forces were still in combat. The maximum sentence possible under the law was five years. Judges in Kentucky pronounced that sentence twice as often as they gave probation. California judges, in the same period, acting under the same federal code, gave sentences of probation to 408 men and maximum sentences of five years imprisonment to two men. In the fifty states one-fourth of all men given maximum sentences were tried in Kentucky which had less than one-sixtieth of the population. Leaving aside the question whether *any* of the sentences were just, we see that obviously gross relative injustice was done because different judges had diverse opinions.

An especially important cause of injustice is the economic class of the offender. Related factors, such as race, education, and age may also affect the ease or difficulty with which the judge identifies with the offender and hence may influence the sentence.

Simon E. Sobeloff, while solicitor general of the United States, described two cases which came before the same court. In one, the cashier of a small bank stole so much money from the bank as to wipe out all its capital and assets. The banker pleaded guilty. The judge suspended sentence and the offender went free. In the other case the same judge gave a sixteen-year-old newsboy eighteen months imprisonment for selling song sheets printed in violation of copyright.

Discrimination against the black and the young in the courts of Philadelphia was made dramatically clear by an investigation of 1971 records. From a seven-month study, the *Philadelphia Inquirer* concluded that "there are two kinds of justice in Philadelphia—one for blacks and one for whites and one for persons under 30 and one for persons older than 30. . . ." The *Inquirer* found also that habitual offenders, because "wise in the ways of the system," were more likely to get out on bail quickly, often committing new crimes while awaiting trial. On the other hand, innocent people without resources "sit for months in jail unable to post bond while awaiting trials that will clear them."

Economic status profoundly affects the treatment of offenders in other ways also. This is particularly obvious when the sentence is a substantial fine. As former Justice Arthur Goldberg comments, "The 'choice' of paying $100 fine or spending thirty days in jail is really no choice at all to the person who cannot raise $100." Imprisonment for lack of money to pay a fine is by no means rare. In fact, the President's Crime Commission reported that 69% of the people confined in local jails were there because they did not have money to pay their fines. Are a man who pays a $100 fine, representing for him one day's income, and a poor man who must spend thirty days in jail for the same offense being treated as equals before the law?

Many inmates of our prisons have seen ringleaders of the crimes in which they participated set free while they themselves must spend years of deprivation caged in an overcrowded bastille. They know well what is the reason. The experienced criminal "big shot" had enough money to retain a good lawyer and corrupt a key prosecutor or witness or else to get a good bargain in negotiating a plea of guilty. The underling in prison is vowing that "next time" he will pull off a big enough job so that he will have the benefits which money can buy. The system of criminal justice conveys to many offenders the message that the important thing is not what you do but how much money you have.

Plea bargaining is an especially bad source of injustice. If a lawbreaker is vice-president of the United States or has money to engage a resourceful lawyer and well-placed friends to bring pressures in the right places, the process of negotiating terms for a plea of guilty can often provide an escape from conviction of a serious crime actually committed. Failing that, the process can usually get such a person a real bargain in the form of a light sentence. On the other hand, if the defendant is poor and badly educated, cannot raise bail to get out of jail while awaiting trial and must depend on a public defender or court-appointed lawyer whose time is divided among a large number of other defendants, the result of a negotiated plea may be disastrous.

Studies have shown that in recent years nearly 90% of persons convicted have pleaded guilty without trial. Most of them have done so after their lawyers have met with prosecutors and agreed on charges to which a guilty plea would be signed and the sentence which the prosecutor would ask of the judge. Often the court then does little but rubber-stamp the agreement. The writer visited a courtroom in Jackson, Mississippi, one day when five criminal cases were disposed of in twenty minutes. The judge sentenced the five people in unrelated cases by reading the papers handed to him by the prosecutor, without so much as looking at any of the defendants while doing so.

Why do not accused persons insist on the public trial which the Constitution guarantees as their right? It is because their attorneys tell them that the deal made with the prosecutor's office is better than they can probably get in open court. It may be. It is known that many judges resent the burden of trials on their own time and the public money. They therefore sentence more heavily defendants who plead innocent than those who plead guilty. Sometimes they argue also that when a person admits his guilt he has taken the first step in rehabilitation. That, however, is a lame argument, considering the motives at work in the process of entering a negotiated plea of guilty. Judges and others frequently say that if all criminal cases went to public trial the courts would be hopelessly swamped with work. In Chapter 16, we must look into this. At present we are noting the injustice which exists in the system as it is.

Not only does plea bargaining result in extremely unequal justice. Occasionally it results in the conviction of innocent people. Consider the plight of a poor man who is accused of a burglary, but who actually had nothing to do with it. He cannot pay for a bail bond and is awaiting trial in jail. The lawyer assigned to him tells him that if he pleads innocent his case will probably not come to trial for six or eight months. Meanwhile, he will stay in jail. If he will plead guilty, the lawyer thinks he can get him a sentence, as a first offender, for no more than six months. In much less time than that he will be eligible for parole. In fact, he may be eligible right away, since he has already been in jail awaiting trial for two months and that time might be counted. Then he can go home to his family and back to his job. "But I didn't do it," he insists. "It's your decision," says the lawyer. "You can wait it out in jail if you want to do it that way." He decides to sign the guilty plea. He now has a record. Later the person actually guilty is found and convicted. But the victim of plea bargaining does not get back the time lost in jail and many people who knew he pleaded guilty to burglary will never believe the later reports, if they so much as hear them. In their minds he will always be a confessed criminal.

5. The Waste of Corrections

Most Americans who have not been inmates know little about jails or prisons. Citizens call for more people to be put into them and want the prisoners kept for longer times, but do not investigate to learn what they are talking about. Some judges make a practice of visiting regularly all the institutions to which they sentence offenders. But such judges are few. Many others have never been inside any of them. We put people behind walls to get them out of our sight and out of our minds. If we suspected that the jails and prisons were the colossal, wasteful failures they are, we would demand to know more and we would then insist on basic changes in the system.

Financial Costs of Corrections.

It is usually harder to get needed funds for corrections than for any other department of government. Who wants to spend

money on criminals? What pride can a sponsor take in such grim monuments as prisons?

Yet people do want protection from criminals, so prisons are used. The more forbidding and invulnerable they look the better the citizenry seems pleased. The high walls and armed guards between a prison population and the public outside give the average citizen a feeling of security. Hence most correctional appropriations go into prisons and to similar institutions for juveniles.

The feeling of security is illusory, because, as we have seen, fewer than 5% of serious crimes are followed by anyone being arrested, convicted, and incarcerated. A much smaller percentage of people who have at some time committed serious crimes are locked up at any one time. Besides, one-third or more of such crimes committed tonight will be done by people who, so far as we know, have never done any such thing before.

Twice as many adult and juvenile offenders are on probation or parole in the community as are in prisons or jails. Yet the expenditures for the prisons and jails are over four times those for control and assistance in the community. Many of the prisons are old, badly run down, and chronically overcrowded. If they are replaced by similar structures the expense will be a heavy burden. Wherever any government is considering such replacement or the building of additional structures, citizens should demand an accounting. When they see what we are getting for the two and one-half billion dollars per year we now pay for corrections, they will demand a drastic change of focus.

We must ask what we are seeking to accomplish by our correctional system. If we want to cause the people in the imprisoned sample of criminal offenders to experience personal indignities, loss of freedom, separation from families and friends, simply as retribution, then that is being accomplished. Sometimes this purpose is described as making the criminal "pay his debt to society." However, it is a curious way of paying a debt. If we include in the taxpayers' costs the constructing and amortizing of buildings, maintaining on welfare the families of those prisoners who were formerly supporting them, the pay of all the staff personnel and other items, the total average price tag for keeping a man in prison for a year comes to above $10,000. If the prisoner is paying a debt to society it is costing the creditor ten grand per year to collect it!

What does society receive in return?

Present Ineffectiveness.

If the correctional system is intended to protect law-abiding citizens from crime, it is almost incredibly ineffective. We have seen how small a proportion of criminal offenders are even caught, let alone convicted and incarcerated. But does not imprisonment turn the criminals away from crime? Judge for your-self a few known facts.

The official National Advisory Commission on Criminal Justice Standards and Goals reported in 1973 an interesting observation. In 1963, the Gideon decision of the United States Supreme Court ruled that under the Constitution every defendant in a criminal trial had a right to legal counsel. As a result of that decision over 1,000 inmates in the Florida prison system were ordered released. Alarmed citizens warned that a terrible crime wave would result. Careful research was done to discover the actual effect. Two groups of inmates, with similar records, released at the same time were matched. The only significant difference was that all in one group had been abruptly released as a result of the Gideon decision. All in the other group were released because they had completed serving their sentences or a normal propor-tion of those sentences. Over a period of two and one-half years, 13.6% of the Gideon group were convicted of new crimes. Of the other group 25.4% or nearly twice as many had new con-victions.

The records of California in a program of greatly widened use of probation in the convicts' home counties instead of imprison-ment by the state gave evidence that convicted offenders placed in prison are less likely to turn away from crime than others who are provided some supervision and assistance—at a fraction of the cost—in their own communities. There are many similar experiences.

The National Advisory Commission reports, "There is substan-tial evidence that probation, fines, public service requirements, and restitution are less costly than incarceration and consistently produce lower rates of recidivism after completion of sentence." From such a conservative source as Norman Carlson, the Director of the Federal Bureau of Prisons, we have the flat statement that prisons are a failure.

Why is this? The search for an answer discloses that they not only fail to accomplish their positive purpose, but are positively evil.

Prisons Dehumanizing.

Physical brutality by American prison guards has, by all accounts, diminished substantially since the early years of this century. Yet in many prisons guards still beat prisoners frequently and mercilessly for disobedience, lack of respect or other offenses, especially if the offender is relatively friendless and powerless, both inside and outside the institution. Guards, now usually called correctional officers, are poorly paid and the work of maintaining security in a prison is not pleasant for a healthy-minded person. Training is usually minimal. Disproportionate numbers of people in such work have limited education, and enjoy holding power over other people. Many are like the more violence-prone inmates they guard in tending to solve their problems by aggressive force.

In *The Crime of Punishment,* Karl Menninger documents many recent brutal practices in American prisons and prison camps, including such tortures as we usually associate with distant places and times centuries past. Recent news accounts have reported the literal torturing to death of a seventeen-year-old first offender in the notorious Cummins Prison Farm of Arkansas; the merciless bludgeoning of prisoners at Attica, New York, both before and after the revolt and its murderous suppression; solitary confinement for months on end; needed medical attention refused; and inmates left in cells with no clothing, toilet facilities, bedding, or light.

The hardened criminal is lacking in adequate sensitive humanity. Prisons seem as if they were designed to complete his dehumanization. Many people first come into prison selfish, aggressive, and badly adapted to life in their communities, but still very human. Sociable, witty, quick in sympathy and help toward a suffering neighbor, many are far from the popular image of "the criminal," despite their episodes of criminal behavior. How do we cultivate their humanity in prison?

They need to learn responsible decision making: we deprive them of opportunity to make even petty decisions as we regiment nearly every move. We say they must be changed: we set them in an unchanging routine for days, months, years. If they are to live as free citizens in the future they must learn to live in the world outside: we cut them off from nearly all contact with the outside world. Their gentler sensibilities need cultivation: the prison limits to a minimum all contacts with family or friends they love. They must learn to respect other persons and their rights: nearly all their contacts are with other criminals or with officers who, in most prisons, show little respect for their rights. We would teach them the satisfaction of honest work and self-support: prisons in the United States usually offer one dollar a day or less, and most of the work is of kinds or with equipment unlike anything outside and so does not prepare them for employment after release.

Prison Society.

A parent who wants sons and daughters to grow up as good persons desires good companions for them. Yet when we want an offender to develop good character we put him into the company of rapists, thieves, robbers, murderers, and child abusers, many of whose activities initially fill him with loathing. During his prison term these will be his cellmates and comrades, the people with whom physical presence and similar plight compel him to find common ground of friendship. With them the one uniting bond is the need to survive under the torments of incarceration. Together they feed on their hostility to the law and the social order which are oppressing them. Many readily admit that for their deeds they deserved punishment. But the longer they are kept inside the walls, the more that connection fades into the background. What remains is the constant, oppressive, demeaning atmosphere and the common alienating struggle against it.

The experience of confinement in selected antisocial company is especially poisonous to all the better impulses of the young. It should not surprise us that the most hardened and dangerous residents of our prisons and of our city streets are usually the graduates of many years in confinement with other offenders, beginning when they were very young, usually before the age of sixteen and often four or more years earlier.

The injustice, ineffectiveness, and destructive influences of our criminal justice system are so pervasive and deeply rooted that we must wonder what purpose it was meant to serve. The fact is that there is no one, rational purpose and this is a principal problem. Successive national commissions have concluded that one trouble with the criminal justice system in the United States was that different agencies in it were seeking different goals and even the same agencies were trying to go in different directions at once. The result is a mass of confusion and self-defeat, a "nonsystem" as the American Bar Association has called it. We need to look carefully at these various purposes if we are to understand what we are seeking when we ask for justice.

6. Conflict and Confusion of Purpose

Justice as Mere Conformity to Law: Legal Positivism.

"It is the law. All the arguments whether marijuana is harmful or not are beside the point. Using marijuana is illegal and when people use it they should be punished." This was sidewalk

comment on an argument before a state legislature for reducing
the penalties for possessing marijuana. According to this view,
justice is whatever the law requires and that is all there is to it.

When one recalls all the frightful things which have been commanded by governments—the crucifixion of Jesus, the torture and
killing of heretics in the Spanish Inquisition, the hanging of
"witches" in Salem, the Nazi massacres of the Jews—one doubts
that many people, when pressed, would hold to this position
without basic modification. It may still be a rallying cry for opposing some kinds of "natural law" theory. But we do not have
to believe that it is the task of every legislature and court to

discover a changeless set of preexisting norms and simply repro-
duce them in human law to recognize that there are at least some
official acts and policies which are flagrantly unjust. That recog-
nition might serve to point toward some broad positive principles
of justice.

Vindication or Effective Declaration of Law.

"If you just say people shouldn't steal, nobody is going to take
it seriously. You have to say it loud and clear by punishing the
people who do it." These words express the theory that justice
is the kind of action by society which will show that some standards of conduct are meant very seriously.

Probably all would agree that one requirement of a just sentence is that it express the seriousness of the law which has been
violated. Yet there are moral standards which would be unfit
subjects for criminal law—for example the love of an adult for
aging parents. The theory of vindication does not go far enough
to tell us much about the criminal laws we should have nor what
results should be sought in the pronouncing of sentence upon
violators.

Retribution.

"Perhaps the death penalty does not reduce the number of
murders. But if a man hits me and breaks my jaw, by golly, I am
going to hit him and try to break his jaw. When a man kills some-
body in cold blood, the state ought to kill him." This is the near-
verbatim argument used by a member of the Maryland House of
Representatives in a corridor discussion after a hearing on his
bill to restore capital punishment.

The theory of vindictive retribution is embedded deep in the
literature and feeling of humankind. Its best-known expression is
the ancient biblical word, "life for life, eye for eye, tooth for

tooth . . ." (Exod. 21:23). There are parallels in other ancient codes of law. Even today, in this country, the public probably gives this idea of equalizing pain and guilt greater prominence than any other idea of justice.

Jesus directly denounced the ancient law (Matt. 5:28–29). At about the same time, authoritative Jewish rabbis were beginning to reinterpret the law of retaliation to require proportionate limitation of punishment. For over sixteen centuries Jewish authorities have taught that monetary fines and other moderate punishments should be used in place of maiming or the death penalty.

Is it not presumptuous for a human being, whether judge, prosecutor or legislator, to think he can judge the measure of subjective moral guilt of another person? Can anyone but God do that? Supposing that we did know just how responsibly guilty was a person's will, how would we arrive at an amount of suffering equivalent to that? If we could, would any good be accomplished by inflicting it? Someone may reply that there is the value of teaching both the culprit and others not to repeat the criminal act. That reply turns attention away from retribution to deterrence.

Deterrence.

"Robberies are increasing in my district. I am making an example of these people who are convicted in my court by giving them the maximum prison terms under the law."

A judge said this during the 1973 graduate course on sentencing in the National College of the State Judiciary, a course which I took with the judges. His honor was expressing the purpose known as general deterrence. A penalty assigned in order that fear may prevent the same person from repeating his crime is special deterrence. In either case it is believed that fear of punishment will turn people away from crime.

Experience shows that punishment which is highly probable,

prompt and moderate does considerably deter people from some offenses of certain kinds. The crimes deterred by fear of punishment are the more deliberate, rational acts done by people accustomed to looking ahead and choosing their way in view of probable consequences. White collar crimes are the most effectively deterred by punishment. Most people drive their cars more lawfully when there are traffic police on the road. Experience has demonstrated that tax evasion is reduced in federal districts where many evaders are caught and are given short sentences of imprisonment, as well as fines and the usual requirements of penalty payments. Unfortunately, white collar crimes are the ones least often penalized to a degree likely to deter. A $10,000 fine for a banker who has embezzled $200,000 is not well calculated to deter him or others from such offenses.

Most Index crimes, on the other hand, are committed by people who, because of drug addiction, desperation, passionate anger, or simply a life-style of living for the moment, do not think much about long-range consequences of their acts. Moreover, the time between an offense and its punishment is likely to be so long and the chances of escaping punishment altogether are so high that deterrent value would be low, even if the potential offenders were longheaded planners as most of them are not.

As observed earlier, the death penalty has been demonstrated to be not only ineffective as a deterrent but actually to produce a slight increase in criminal homicides when it is used. Probably this is due to a combination of subconscious suicidal desire ("death wish") of some, playing on morbid imaginings of others, and an intensifying of hostility in the minds of people who tend to feel identified with the executed person. Why the death penalty incites slightly more murders than it prevents by deterrence, we do not know with certainty, but the truth that it does so has been demonstrated in too many times and places to be doubted any longer by anyone who knows the data and is sufficiently realistic to look at facts rather than unsupported theory and mere appeals to emotion.

Disablement.

"Every time he gets out on the street he soon goes back to his old trade as a burglar. He will have to be taken out of circulation for a good long time."

The judge speaking does not have any confidence that repeated punishment will deter this particular offender from further burglaries. He has decided that the only way he can protect the community from his thieving activities is to put him behind prison walls for a long period. Then he will be unable to ply his criminal trade for that length of time.

There are other methods of incapacitation which accomplish the purpose of preventing some kinds of crimes. For example, a lawyer who betrays his trust may be disbarred. A banker who embezzles funds may be forbidden by terms of probation to resume the holding of other people's money. A labor leader who has misused union funds has been forbidden to hold union office again. A reckless or drunken driver may lose his license to drive. Lifting his license, however, may not be effective in a jurisdiction where road checks are infrequent. One Maryland man, who is now serving one of his various sentences for drunken driving and operating without a license, is nearly forty and says he has been driving frequently since he was sixteen, although he has never held a license since he was arrested at seventeen for drunken driving. In his case, if his story is true, disablement has not been very effective excepting in the periods of his incarceration. Rapists and child abusers have sometimes been surgically unsexed to disable them. Unfortunately, hostile aggressiveness motivating their criminal activities has then found new channels of expression, including aggravated assault and murder.

Obviously, we must choose with great care the methods to be

used for the disabling of criminal offenders and we must recognize the limitations of this purpose. However, few readers will doubt that some methods of disabling for some crimes should be used.

Rehabilitation.

"What good will it do to put her in prison? Her problem is getting drunk and then doing these reckless things. She needs help with her alcohol problem."

When a judge expressed this opinion he was supporting the aim of rehabilitation, undoubtedly the purpose most often commended among people having humane and rational concerns for both offenders and the public. The argument for it is simple. Nearly all the people now in jails and prisons will be free some day. They will then be likely to commit crime again unless meanwhile they develop the attitudes and habits of law-abiding citizens. Therefore, correctional officers should do their utmost to reform the inmates in their institutions.

Although the argument carries much weight, it is less decisive than it looks at first sight. Some prison inmates disobeyed laws no longer operative, such as conscription laws in wartime or laws against gambling later repealed. Since they showed no inclination to disobey other laws they may need no reforming to live as law-abiding citizens. Other inmates committed single offenses in extraordinary circumstances which rarely occur in any human lives and are extremely unlikely or even impossible to occur again in these particular lives. Finally, even when reform would be needed to turn an inmate to a law-abiding citizenship, it does not necessarily follow that officials or any other persons know what policy or program would accomplish such a purpose. There are, in fact several different modes of rehabilitation being proposed and, in places, practiced.

Education is one. Noting that the average prison inmate is a

scarcely literate school dropout, we can readily see that his lack
of education will be a handicap to him when he is released. Many
prisons and some jails have programs of education through which
a few inmates increase knowledge and reading skills, sometimes
taking examinations for certificates of high school equivalency.
Much smaller numbers similarly earn college credits. Such efforts
are certainly commendable, but success in them does not correlate
impressively with going straight after parole or release.

Vocational education is recommended in order that ex-offenders will establish working habits and satisfactions and have means
of honest support when they leave the walls. Many do help themselves by such means. But courses available inside usually fail
to match both the positive interest of a particular inmate and
his opportunities for employment outside. The inmates who do
become self-supporting and law-abiding citizens usually work in
jobs unrelated to their prison courses of vocational training.

Therapy of various kinds, from group sessions of Alcoholics
Anonymous to full treatment by a psychiatrist (rare) is used in
many institutions. Results are often good when the therapist or
group leader is a person of realistic but compassionate concern,
who respects the human dignity of each inmate as a person. Yet
again the large majority of inmates do not respond well to therapy
nor demonstrate that they have been helped by it.

Religious conversion is pushed by evangelistic preachers and
Black Muslims, alike. Many persons do, through conversion and
religious instruction, gain new insights, life goals, and experiences of divine assistance through which they rebuild their lives.
While such changes can be offered, they cannot be forced and
most of the inmates refuse them.

Behavior modification is in recent vogue, under the influence of
writings from B. F. Skinner. Like other terms which become
fashionable, this one has taken on such a variety of meanings as
to become almost useless. Its original and more distinctive meaning, however, is directed to changing the overt behavior of a

person without concern about such subjective experiences as conscience, motives, purposes, and the like. It uses "aversion" therapy in which the person is given short-term and immediate discomfort whenever he starts to do something which the staff disapprove, while the "reinforcement" of pleasurable rewards comes whenever he displays approved behavior.

Some elements of behavior modification are used in all situations where some short-term control must be exercised. But standing alone, as means of changing a person's life-style, it has proved to be a dismal failure—for example at the federal Robert F. Kennedy Youth Center. Many youth who learned to manipulate the system for quick rewards there have later illegally manipulated forces operating on the street for other short-term rewards.

The preponderant evidence indicates that to make constructive and permanent changes in a person's conduct he must be respected as a person and his cooperation won. We do not get good results by treating him like a machine to be adjusted or like one of the pigeons on which Skinner experimented.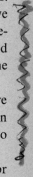

Character education of various kinds has been tried. The more promising modes involve carefully planned social groupings in which different inmates learn to depend on each other and so to be responsible to each other.

It seems clear that no one approach will meet the needs or improve the conduct of all the widely different persons in a jail or prison. All who study the various programs of rehabilitation learn also that a typical American prison is one of the most unlikely places we could find to rehabilitate anyone for responsible living.

Combination of Purposes.

We have now reviewed briefly the more common ideas concerning the meaning and purpose of criminal justice. Some combination of them seems to be required. Perhaps you would join me in rejecting retribution. No one can know the moral guilt of another. Even if we could know that, it is absurd to think we could define a certain amount of suffering equal to the guilt. If we could somehow determine this amount, it would still be wrong to inflict such suffering unless some good could be accomplished by it. We will return to this subject in Chapter 14. If we do seek some future good to be accomplished by sentencing a convicted person, then we have adopted another purpose instead of retribution—be it deterrence, disablement, rehabilitation, or some other. Of these last three all appear to have their rightful places, while none is entitled to be dominant in all cases.

We will need some whole, inclusive aim for the criminal justice system. If such an aim is to be adopted and satisfactorily employed in the United States it must be deeply rooted in the American pluralistic heritage.

We have noticed that this country has both by far the greatest volume of violent crime among the developed countries of the West and also the harshest system for punishing the relatively few criminals we catch and convict. If we are to see how we ought to change our system, we need to understand the historic and cultural roots both of our high crime rate and of our harsh system of justice. As we look at these roots, we shall find also, in our American heritage, rich resources for better things.

QUESTIONS FOR THOUGHT

1. Considering what you know about the present system of criminal justice, do you think you should report to the police crimes which you observe? In every instance?

2. If you report a crime have you any further obligations in the matter?

3. Do you think your local and state police are honest and fair? If you are a white, middle-class adult, ask some high school teen-agers and young collegians what they think. Also ask some members of minority groups—black, Spanish-speaking, Asian, or American Indian—whether they find the police to be fair in distributing their services and in enforcing the laws.

4. Have your local and state police published regulations which state clearly the duties and the standards for promotion of police officers? If not try to find the actual working standards. Do you approve them?

5. Are there any laws of local government or state or nation which seem to you clearly unjust? Why? Does injustice in the laws reflect similar bias in social relationships and personal attitudes in the community?

6. Arrange to go with another member of your study group or a friend and neighbor to observe proceedings in a criminal court through some cases not widely publicized. If there are occurrences you do not understand, ask a court officer or the judge to explain. Do you like what you see and hear? Why?

7. How many arrests of juveniles do your police make? What are the proportions of boys and of girls involved? What are the more frequent offenses for which boys are charged with delinquency? Girls? How do the police handle them?

8. On what charges are adults most frequently arrested in your city, county or state? What is the usual disposition of these cases? Is the outcome useful?

9. In your state how much money goes into corrections? What proportion of the funds goes to institutions and what proportion to field services of probation and parole? What are the numbers of inmates of institutions? The numbers of convicted persons under the treatment of field services?

10. Arrange to visit a prison, perhaps to attend a religious service or some other kind of inmates' meeting to which outsiders are admitted, such as Jaycees, Alcoholics Anonymous, or Seventh Step. How does the visit affect your conception of prisons and of criminals?

SUGGESTED FURTHER READING

Ask the Chamber of Commerce of the United States for their latest free pamphlet on modernizing corrections.

Karl Menninger, M.D., *The Crime of Punishment*. Paperback. New York: The Viking Press, 1968.

Marvin E. Frankel, *Criminal Sentencing. Law Without Order*. New York: Hill and Wang, 1973.

Gus Tyler, *Organized Crime in America: A Book of Readings*. Paperback. Ann Arbor: The University of Michigan, 1971.

7. Origins

Puritan Benevolence and Hardness.

"A strange hybrid, indeed, did circumstances beget here in the New World, upon the old Puritan stock, and the earth never before saw such mystic-practicalism, such niggard-geniality, such calculating-fanaticism, such cast-iron-enthusiasm, such sour-faced-humor, such close-fisted-generosity" (James Russell Lowell). Undoubtedly, every nation, and especially every large one, has contrary inclinations and ideals within its culture. The United States, however, holds to sharply contrasting norms with unusual tenacity. We not only fail to resolve the resulting tensions, but ardently promote opposing ideals as moral obligations. The opposites are often defended by the same people.

We have noted the uniqueness of the United States in the amount and seriousness of violent crime and also the unusual severity and inconsistency with which we punish criminal offenders. We can understand the futility of our efforts to control crime only as we become aware of the opposing strands in our cultural heritage.

Most of our American forebears were selected or selected themselves as among the most aggressive and discontented people in the Old World. Some were in serious trouble with the law

and either fled or were expelled. Much larger numbers were so
seriously dissatisfied with religious, political, or economic conditions at home that they underwent great risks to solvency and to
life itself by embarking on the adventure of colonization in America. When they came, their neighbors of more placid tempera-
ment remained east of the Atlantic. Most of our immigrant ancestors, then, were aggressive malcontents. Is it strange that we are
more restless, discontented, and aggressive than most peoples?

The immigrants from Africa were, of course, tragic exceptions,
since nearly all were brought against their wills. However, much
more than the Europeans, they were broken off from their cul-

tural roots. With tribal and family connections broken and native tongues rendered useless, the slaves were left forlorn, detached individuals, dependent upon the culture of people who looked upon them as scarcely human. It is small wonder that their descendants find it difficult or impossible to identify themselves with the culture which has perpetrated such savage cruelty upon them. Under the circumstances, it is remarkable that they have contributed so much as they have to the majority culture.

The original Americans have been permitted to contribute very little to the dominant society. The Indians, at best, have faced the choice of submerging themselves as individuals in the customs and institutions of the white immigrants, thus giving up their "Indianism," or accepting places in reservations deliberately barred from genuine participation in the wider society.

The formation of ideals and institutions which have shaped the effective legal conscience of America has been almost exclusively the work of European immigrants. In that work, English Puritans, including Separatists, Puritan Anglicans, and Calvinistic nonconformists, along with religiously similar Calvinists of the Continental Reformed and Scotch Presbyterian churches, have played the dominant roles. Especially was this so in the formative colonial years.

Two beliefs made the influence of Puritanism on the law especially strong. One was the conviction that a stern rule of law was necessary to the survival of any human society. Since all people were totally depraved, they would destroy the social order if not strictly restrained. The second was the belief that the laws of the state should conform wholly to the laws of God as set forth in the biblical Books of Law and interpreted by his ministers. Indeed, under Puritan dominance, the Connecticut Colony used the Mosaic Code as its only law for twenty-four years.

The Puritans who came to Massachusetts were determined to found an ideal commonwealth, the everyday life of which would be a model for all the world. They began even before their arrival to form a closely cooperative community characterized by much benevolence and mutual helpfulness.

Something went wrong quickly. They felt deeply that their precarious colony was preserved only by God's will. If they were to continue under his guardianship they must live in that ideal commonwealth which he had commanded them to form. But God's law was frequently violated. People failed to go to church; they stole; they taught false doctrines; they practiced fornication and adultery. All such conduct threatened the very existence of the colony and all the people in it, since it constituted violation of their covenant with God. Believing in law, as they did, they were sure that they must deal legally and sternly with every kind of sin and heresy, in order to root out the evil.

The ideals held by the Puritans led to much voluntary benevolence and even to the forming of socialistic communities. Land was owned and cultivated by the whole community in the earliest years of both Plymouth and Jamestown. Later, under similar religious motivation, more than 120 such communities were formed including such famous ones as New Harmony, Oneida, and Brook Farm. Much more lasting and widespread have been the voluntarily supported hospitals, colleges, agencies for domestic and foreign relief, and many other causes.

On the other hand, the literal biblicism and the almost desperate determination to maintain a holy commonwealth pure in life and doctrine, led to vindictive intolerance and much cruelty. The ministers urged on the harsh legalism, scolding the governors and magistrates when they failed to take "a life for a life" (Exod. 21:23), and solemnly condemning all departures from the doctrines they preached.

Virginia, under rule of the Virginia Company (1607–1624), enforced observance of the Sabbath even more rigorously than New England. In the Virginia of those days, saying anything against teachings of the Bible or against the Anglican Articles of Religion was punishable by death. Even the frequently praised "Maryland Toleration Act" provides that anyone who denies the doctrine of the Holy Trinity or denies that Jesus is the Son of God "shall be punished with death and confiscation or forfeiture of all his or her land and goods. . . ." As Roman Catholic Maryland demonstrated, the Puritans were not the only people of narrowly limited tolerance, but they bear especially heavy responsibility because of their greater degree of harsh legalism and their larger influence on American law and conscience.

The paradox of generous lovingkindness and harsh cruelty within the colonial communities gave rise to much uneasiness and tension. Such people as Anne Hutchinson, Roger Williams, and the Quakers vigorously protested against the severe intolerance. Death penalties prescribed by law for minor offenses were seldom if ever employed, despite urgings by some clergy. The ministers and the churches suffered a severe setback in public esteem in a backlash against the execution of witches at Salem. Nevertheless, the harsh side of the paradox was deeply planted and other forces were to cultivate it in time.

Paradox in the Great Awakening.

The series of religious revivals known as the Great Awakening swept through all the colonies between 1738 and the Revolution. Its two greatest figures, Jonathan Edwards and George Whitefield, left an especially profound impression as the colonies moved toward the birth of the United States as an independent nation.

Edwards was one of the greatest intellects of American history. He combined an idealistic philosophy with Calvinistic theology in new ways which moderated the rigors of Calvinism while at the same time perpetuating and extending its influence. He also helped to give the Great Awakening a positive attitude toward higher education. From New England down the East Coast and, later, all across the country, colleges and universities were formed in the wake of the religious revivals. Some institutions have continued church relationships, while many have become wholly independent. In both categories are many of the most influential schools of the nation.

George Whitefield, more than any other one person, was responsible for carrying the religious revival through all the colonies. Historians grant him considerable credit for giving to the people of all sections a sense of unity transcending loyalty to their individual colonies and states. Also, the new sense of independent personal dignity, derived from experiences of God's grace, undergirded movement toward a more inclusive democracy and also toward the demand for independence from Great Britain.

The Great Awakening continued the dual development of contrary cultural trends and spread them more thoroughly over the land. On the one hand, most of the ministers and churches leading it shared the basic ideas of Puritanism—the absolute sovereignty of God, the authority of the whole Bible, strict requirements of personal conduct, belief in thrift and hard work and intolerance of contrary teaching. On the other hand, as converts were exhorted to improve themselves by hard study and new colleges flourished, the humane and generous themes of the intellectual Enlightenment also gained strength. These more liberal results of the revivals blended with the secular political philosophies of men like Benjamin Franklin, James Madison, George Mason, and Thomas Jefferson, strengthening the democratic sentiments of tolerance and humane generosity.

Thomas Jefferson.

Anyone who would understand the cultural context of American law must take into account the principal author of the Declaration of Independence, our third president, who was also an especially influential writer on the philosophy of government.

The best-known and most important single writer exerting influence on Jefferson was John Locke, whose very phrases appear at critically important points in the Declaration of Independence. Locke especially affected Jefferson's doctrines of human equality and the responsibility of government to support natural law rights, including the right of revolution against tyranny.

Jefferson tried to moderate penalties against crime in Virginia and had limited success. His humane principles were reinforced by the writings of Italy's Cesare Beccaria (1738–1794), who opposed retributive punishment and urged respect for the humanity of criminals. Jefferson called the "eye-for-eye" *lex talionis* a "revolting principle."

One of the worst and most pervasive features of criminal justice as practiced in America is the unequal treatment of the rich and powerful as over against the poor and weak. Jefferson had an important part in developing the uneasy conscience of Americans relative to such inequality. When he wrote that "all men are created equal," he meant to assert, as his letters make clear, that, regardless of abilities or race, all were equal in the rights to life, liberty, and the pursuit of happiness.

Jefferson included in his original draft of the Declaration a ringing denunciation of the slave trade, showing clearly that black people should be included in the equal rights so memorably affirmed. Unfortunately, his own practice did not measure up to his rhetoric, for he continued to hold slaves to the end of his life.

His practice of slavery, in contrast to his eloquent condemnations of it, has generated much recent discussion. It is true that he tried to push through the Virginia legislature a bill to permit slaveowners to free their slaves voluntarily and without such a law he probably could not have made his slaves free. Yet he surely could have so changed the conditions of their employment at Monticello that they would have been in fact hired servants, even though they would not have been able to go away and be recognized as free citizens. For all his reputed generous kindness to his slaves, he still built his own prosperity on slave labor. He left no doubt that he wanted to see all slaves liberated, but he believed that they should be settled as freemen elsewhere, preferably in Africa, since he thought that people of the two races could not happily live together in a common citizenship.

On the whole, Jefferson's tolerant, humane writings have left a deeper imprint than his inconsistent practice, and have been cited many times by champions of civil rights. Yet many of his more advanced proposals were regularly defeated and his own life did not escape the evils which, as he recognized, damaged the lives of slaveholders as well as slaves. The vicious inhumanity of slavery was joined by other forces which, during the 19th century, would further strengthen aggressive individualism, release new violence, and develop more illusions of power and self-righteousness.

The better influences of the Great Awakening and Jeffersonian humanism would persist in the American psyche and find frequent expression. But the opposing forces of ruthless individualism and the drive for wealth and power would be mightily reinforced and leave to the 20th century a dark heritage nearly unmanageable in its later decades.

8. The Rush for Riches

European farmers were being squeezed into ever smaller plots as population increased in the 17th, 18th, and 19th centuries. Other laboring people saw no chance to escape poverty in the Old World. The vast empty areas of land in America, much of it good land, powerfully attracted large numbers of such people. Much of the promotional literature featured the prospect of land for the taking.

In the first century of colonization, poor soil—especially in New England—and distance from markets limited money-making possibilities. The Indian occupants of the land also chilled the fervor of many colonists by their fierce resistance and counter-attacks against the invaders. Moreover, the Puritans and many others brought with them class structures in which they had formerly lived. Leaders sought to dissuade people of the lower classes from moving upward alongside people of higher class. Climbing often took place nevertheless, but the old social structures changed so slowly that there was little disruption of social stability.

The colonists in most areas made more money by land speculation than any other method, through the 18th century. The person who arrived first, grabbed the most good land, and de-

fended it most successfully reaped rich rewards. So did the one who took his profits to buy up land while it was cheap, then sold it after increasing settlement and scarcity drove up the price.

After the War of Independence, the drive to conquer the wilderness rose to a high pitch and continued throughout the 19th century. As farming and industry became more profitable, the same feverish, competitive drive to get ahead was observed and commented upon by some editors and many European visitors. Before the end of the 18th century the pattern of competitive, capitalistic individualism was well established. Most people in Europe were settled in their own niches and, unless disturbed by war or natural calamity, they lived in a well-structured system of mutual responsibilities, however restricted or unfair. In America, everyone was on his own and after independence was expected to drive ahead as far as his labor and wits would take him.

People in all countries recognize the need for economic production. But material progress of the individual is not generally given such a strongly dominant priority as here.

"The Rat Race."

Gradually the social restraints weakened, as the rewards for individuals who ignored them went higher. The gold rush in 1848 is notorious for the ruthless aggressiveness of the men who grabbed promising plots for prospecting and drove others out by deceit or violence. Often they gambled all their savings and their moral principles as well, in the effort to strike it rich. That was only one episode in the feverish pursuit of wealth which dominated much of the country in the 19th century and has continued on through the 20th. The "robber barons" of the 19th century made vast fortunes from coal, steel, railroads, textiles, tobacco, heavy manufacturing, and oil. They pyramided corporations and by their manipulations squeezed out thousands of small shareholders, many of whom lost their modest life savings. They corrupted government to get vast concessions of land for railroads, mining rights, and oil. Some did then give away large sums to universities, libraries, and benevolent foundations. In the 20th century, oil and natural gas have provided the biggest bonanzas. Nearly half of the recent multimillionaires have gained their fortunes from these sources with a minimum of personal service. The most noteworthy qualities of some have been their lack of education and public concern, their stinginess, their lucky gambles and the ruthlessness with which they have corrupted government and exploited the public for personal gain.

Millions of middle-class people have been caught up in "the rat race" and cannot see any way to escape. Struggling to keep up with their neighbors, their material expectations are so high that there seems no escape from a constant feverish effort to make money. Young business executives confide that they find their moral scruples being eroded as they try to meet the insatiable demands of their companies and superiors to cut corners of honesty and legality for profit. The same demand to "win and win big" which led to Watergate and all the related crimes of the Nixon White House infests many a corporation. Ideals of generous community-mindedness are still held by many of the persons involved and are frequently reinforced as they attend church and subscribe to the teachings of many associations. Yet these ideals are overridden by the demands of material success and a misplaced loyalty to "the game plan" of the business staff, just as among the staff members working under Mr. Nixon.

Breaking Down Social Structures.

Individual loyalty to a self-serving special-interest group is no substitute for basic social structures interwoven with the fabric of a whole community. In countless neighborhoods the basic structures have been fragmented and splintered until little remains but individuals trying to use each other for their own advantage.

A mantle of piety is often cast over this individual pursuit of wealth. "The American way," it is called, or "rugged individualism." Such blessing of it by the secular religion can make the participants feel positively righteous in their selfish materialism. They may scorn, at the same time, the people who have not been inclined or able to keep up the pace.

Americans, like many other people of the present world are predominantly city dwellers. They also move frequently—oftener than once in five years on the average. Conditions of the city and the frequent moving to new homes both aggravate the tendency to individualism and subject all social institutions to severe strain. People who move to a new neighborhood, especially in a city, tend to feel less moral restraint from social pressures, more often feel alienated and more rapidly develop unrelieved and unendurable anxieties and tensions. Whether among ghetto dwellers or middle-class suburbanites, such conditions raise the rate of crime.

The family is especially important to the moral health of the community. It is the first and potentially the strongest line of defense against social disorder and crime. The person growing up without strong family ties is especially likely to develop into a "loner," or to join with others who feel left out and hostile toward the established order. Such alienation and animosity often lead to crime and are exceedingly difficult to change.

The weakening of the family in America is so well known that the point need not be labored here. The high rates of divorce and desertion, the problems of schoolteachers in handling otherwise undisciplined and unguided children, and the number of young couples who are choosing to live together, break up and remate without marriage or divorce are all signs of the embattled family.

Families have taken many effective forms in human history. Especially well known are the traditional larger families in many lands and the older American farm families in which everyone above infancy participated both in earning the livelihood and in household chores. But no orderly society has long existed without a strongly communal family structure of some kind. It is this, and not merely a traditional set of roles, which is now threatened in America by excessive individualism.

In too many homes, father, mother, son, and daughter all look for their pleasures in their own individual ways, in radical disregard of other members. Each one who earns money goes his or her separate way to do it and of course the children go out to their own school classes and peer groups. Many a home becomes little more than a place to sleep most nights and eat most days, often at individually variant hours.

The individualism strong in America from the beginning and reinforced by the rush for riches in a geographically and industrially expanding society, has literally come home. As it undermines and often altogether destroys the family it gains that much more force. When even the family is held together only by the uncertain ties of convergent individual pleasures and material interests, the social order is in serious trouble and high rates of crime are inevitable.

Many people sense that marriage, family, and neighborhood are breaking up and look for the enemy in their midst who is causing the trouble. They turn their anxiety into vindictive anger against the people selected, especially criminal offenders outside the establishment, but also against other groups perceived as deviant from social custom. They call on criminal law to restore the ordered unity of society. When the disorder persists, they call for ever more severe and often for mandatory penalties to impose order by force.

Few observe that the angry calls for the death penalty or

mandatory life sentences arise from motives strikingly similar to the motivation of violent crime itself. Both represent individuals lashing out against other people who are seen as obstructing or threatening their own way of life. Both see the other person as an impersonal thing or an enemy, not as a fellow member of a single human community. Both, alike, further fracture the community.

Division of society into estranged ethnic communities plays an especially important part in the high rate of crime and in the vindictive reactions to it. We now turn to this subject.

9. Race, National Origin, and Violence

The Indians.

White Americans, who think of themselves as a peaceful and honorable people, have shown to the indigenous population such wanton violence, perfidy, impatient greed, and cruelty as belie the most rudimentary professions of civilized conduct. Helen Hunt Jackson's partial exposure of the record in 1881, under the title *A Century of Dishonor* might well be extended to cover three centuries of broken treaties and violated human rights.

William Penn and the Quakers demonstrated that it was possible to build a large and eminently successful colony on mutual understanding and fair compensation, with no fighting or massacres as long as the Quakers maintained control of the white colonizers. At first, the very survival of the Plymouth Colony had depended on the generous hospitality of the Indians. But after the numbers of colonists became so large that they threatened the livelihood of the Indians, the relationship became a kind of uneasy truce, broken by raids and massacres on both sides. Some English settlers protested against the usual assumption that the British throne had a right to assign vast lands to proprietors or companies without regard to prior claims by the inhabitants. One of these protesters, Roger Williams, was expelled for this and other reasons. In Rhode Island he tried to base colonial policy on

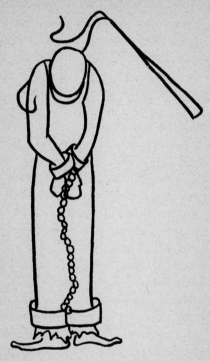

fair and mutually advantageous negotiated agreements. But such consideration was rare.

Even when the white settlers had negotiated for specified lands and guaranteed Indian rights to exclusive occupation and control beyond their limits, it was usually only a short time until those rights were violated as the settlers moved west. The pattern of broken treaties was continuing even into the 1970s.

Earlier, it seemed acceptable to ride roughshod over Indian rights and even to slaughter wantonly the indigenous people because they were widely viewed as subhuman or at least so evil as to have no human rights. Theodore Roosevelt said that he thought at least nine out of ten Indians deserved the old saying that "the only good Indian is a dead Indian." Settlers offered bounties for any Indian scalp as early as 1641 and as late as 1814, when the territory of Indiana made such an offer. No criminal charges of homicide there! No discrimination between hostile or dangerous individuals and unarmed, sleeping, or friendly ones! No horror of barbaric scalping! Any scalp would be paid for by the territory of Indiana so long as it came from an Indian head.

Fights between white settlers and neighboring Indians became legendary. Until the middle of the 20th century, few people pointed out that after the early colonial years, while the Indians might win local skirmishes, in the larger context they faced so much larger numbers and heavier firepower that early disaster was a foregone conclusion. We must not detract from the courage or the magnanimity of white individuals and groups in some particular episodes. But American novels and movies have betrayed the truth and debauched our national character as they have pictured the civilized, heroic cowboys and treacherous, inferior, savage Indians who, in actuality, were trying desperately to defend their homelands and hunting grounds.

In this idealized tradition of gloriously tough character, the good American is ready for quick resort to force, especially gunfire, inclined to take the law into his own hands, and prepared for vindictive response to wrongs, fancied or real. This tradition is now expressed both in a high rate of violent crimes unique among developed nations and in exceptionally harsh treatment of the more powerless convicted offenders.

Slavery and Its Legacy.

The North, especially New England, and the South alike were deeply involved in the inhuman slave trade. The traders corrupted tribal chiefs in Africa to sell their most unpopular or feared subjects or prisoners of war. They packed masses of men, women, and children in the holds of their ships with no privacy or sanitary facilities, with minimal and often unclean food and water. The traders' cruelty seems to have been limited only by their desire not to have so many slaves die in passage as to reduce their net profits.

The survivors of the terrible ocean passage were sold, with much deliberate separation of families, as well as of tribal compatriots, the better to divide and control. Other separations occurred simply for considerations of profit. In 1860, about one of every seven persons in the United States was a slave.

There have been various efforts to support the claim that slavery was only a form of labor relations which, like other forms, was not so bad excepting under individual owners who were cruel. But public documents of law and commerce expose an institution so vile in its denial of elementary human rights as to belie all professions of humanity and reason, let alone talk of Christian love and mercy.

Slaveowners violated the sanctity of marriage for breeding purposes or to satisfy their own lust. They sold children from their mothers and fatherhood was ignored. A Mississippi court ruled that there was no such an offense as the rape of a slave woman. A Kentucky court held that at law there was no such person as the father of a slave.

The heritage of violence from slavery did not end with liberation. The terrible Civil War and the years following Reconstruction added much. A careful study of historical records shows that whether local government by former slaves and their white allies was efficient and fair or not, most of the southern whites regarded participation in government by former slaves as intolerable. Their response to it was the new violence by the Ku Klux Klan and others. Congressional investigation exposed thousands of whippings, mutilations, shootings, and hangings. In the last weeks before the election of 1868 two thousand persons were killed or wounded in Louisiana alone. Only 17% of lynch victims were accused of raping or attempting to rape white women, despite white folklore to the contrary. Rather, most were accused of attempting to vote, engaging in labor union activities and the like.

The whole white experience of dominating black people, using them, pushing them aside and assuming superiority over them has both expressed and increased white Americans' tradition of aggressive, hardhearted ruthlessness. It has had an even more intense effect on black people because it has been concentrated on their much smaller numbers and they have had to live with it constantly. It has affected every aspect of their lives, social, economic, political, and residential.

One effect in both the white and black communities is crime. Because a far larger proportion of whites than of blacks hold positions of influence in our economic and political institutions, the crime tends to take different forms. Crime of the blacks is more often of the Index varieties—the so-called street crimes. Crime of the whites is more often of the white collar varieties.

Which kind of misconduct does more harm to the whole social order? To answer, we should need to weigh the atmosphere of fear and hostility which hangs like a pall over our inner cities against the general distrust of government, resentment against the oil companies and others, enormous waste of resources, the greater volume of economic loss to all Americans, and loss of confidence in the future of America which poisons our national life.

We do not need to answer the comparative question to see the monstrous price in crime, violence, and repression which we are all paying for the long chronic aggression against the black people of America.

Nativism and Later Immigrants.

After Anglo-Saxons established clear dominance, they were able to decide who would be welcome and who would not. At first, most immigrants were welcomed as additions to the supply of labor. This positive attitude continued generally through the great influx of refugees from the Irish famine in the mid-19th century and to the Civil War.

Employers continued to encourage immigration, but the labor unions began to resist it because of the added competition for jobs. As the Irish and Germans, then a great influx from southern and eastern Europe, thronged the ports of entry, opposition spread to the middle and upper classes.

In the last decade of the 19th century many editorials and articles, and some books, praised the vigorous Anglo-Saxon or Teutonic blood of the older American lineages, with their devotion to the strenuous self-reliant life. In contrast to the newer immigrants, the Nordics were praised as heroic fighters, aggressive and eminently fit to rule.

From the beginning such ethnic bias was deeply entangled with anti-Catholicism. This combination came to the surface again in the 1920s and 1930s, with a surge of hostility to all who were not "WASP" (white Anglo-Saxon Protestant). The Ku Klux Klan was reorganized and grew to considerable size before some of its leaders were convicted of misappropriating funds and rising opposition to all it represented reduced it to relative impotence. However, the Klan and the whole anti-immigration movement had mightily reinforced the self-righteous, vindictive and even violently aggressive strain in American tradition.

Idealizing Violence.

It is true that other nations have indulged in episodes of wholesale violence without equal here. Yet the continual frequency of it, its institutionalized and idealized character and its contrast with our professions of national virtue are unique among developed nations of the 20th century.

There are reasons why this tradition has become especially

destructive in the 1960s and 1970s. To understand them fully, we must look at the place of time and space in American culture and in the present scene.

10. Time and Space in America

"It is not too much to say that in America space has played the part that time has played in the older cultures of the world." So writes Sidney E. Mead in *The Lively Experiment* (New York: Harper and Row, 1963). What does this mean?

European Time; American Space.

Any American who lives and works in a European country, even for a short time, is likely to be impressed with the patience of the people. He may be annoyed with their seemingly easygoing ways. In England, especially, the quiet, good-natured waiting of turns in any of the many long queues encountered in an ordinary day is a wonder to American visitors. More marvelous is the rational coolness with which most English people accept more serious disruptions of life, whether from wartime bombing of their cities or from an energy shortage suddenly aggravated, in early 1974, by an oil embargo and then raised to critical proportions by a coal miners' strike. The people generally expect that somehow they will "muddle through" *in time*. Time is a commodity of which there appears to be an adequate supply.

Although most of the earliest American immigrants were from England, they were not typical and the new environment quickly heightened their impatience.

From the beginning, the time has always seemed to Americans already too late. The Pilgrims landed at Plymouth in early winter. They desperately needed houses, a harvest of food, the friendship of the Indians and, in case that should fail, defenses. There was not time enough. Half of them died before they could bring in their first harvest. Americans at Plymouth, Jamestown, New Amsterdam, and even St. Augustine, were dropped on this continent already running to catch up and they have never stopped.

The peoples of Europe, as Mead stresses, had found themselves confined in space. Such freedom as they could find must be dis-

covered in time. American settlers, on the other hand, hard-pressed in time, had plenty of space. The immense areas of unused or sparsely used land gave the illusion of infinite space and resources.

Many people were always eager to move west and claim large tracts of land before others did so. Other people who were pulled along were always struggling to conquer the wilderness, build shelter, and get seed planted. There was never enough time, but there was always space. So much new land was available that for several generations American farmers made little effort to fertilize, plow deeply, or rotate crops. When the thin soil became less productive, the people moved west again and the restless struggle was renewed. When population became congested and problems of city life began to appear, the West beckoned.

Frontier Time and Violence.

The sense of limited time had much to do with violence on the frontier. Time was perceived as too short to permit seemingly endless talks with Indians, to achieve mutual understanding about land use and occupation. Often time seemed lacking even for reaching agreement with white neighbors. The threat or actual use of the gun was faster and speed of solution appeared to be essential.

Likewise, when crime occurred—provisions, cattle, or horses stolen, a wife seduced or a daughter raped—time did not permit judicial sifting of the evidence and thoughtful weighing of penalties. Instead, the "swift justice" of vigilantes forcing the offender to ride out of the county on a sharp rail, the tar and feathering or the shoot-out was the answer adopted.

American Use of Space to Relieve Tensions.

American space was used from the beginning to relieve European stresses. Religious dissenters under pressure to conform and suffering discrimination or even active persecution relieved both themselves and their tormenters by putting the Atlantic Ocean between them. Others were banished to America or, especially in the 19th century, came to escape economic pressures or disasters. Since economic stringencies often produce political upheavals, space on this continent thus served as a safety valve for Europe.

Americans have repeated such processes thousands of times within the area of the United States. In the 17th century, many people suffered from strong pressures to conform, especially, but by no means only, in New England. In later generations we have become willing to accept wider deviance. Yet tolerance in religion and life-style has continued to be limited. Because useful space has been available, people who, like Roger Williams, thought "otherwise" could go away without suffering as a result. Sometimes they were officially commanded to leave or threatened by vigilantes and ordered to "move on."

Thus Anne Hutchinson and John Wheelwright were condemned

in a solemn synod meeting at Newtown in 1637 and banished from Massachusetts Bay in 1638. A Virginia law of 1662 instructed the executive authorities to compel "all nonconformists to depart the colony with all convenience." The Maryland Toleration Act of 1649 specified that banishment was to be the penalty for a third offense of speaking "reproachful words . . . concerning the blessed Virgin Mary . . . or the holy Apostles or Evangelists."

Even in the 1970s a person who has been repeatedly arrested on minor charges, so that he has become a chronic nuisance, may be told by a prosecutor that charges will not be pressed if he moves out of the town, county or state and does not return. During American fighting in Vietnam, the notion that protesting nonconformists should go away was expressed in the sign displayed on many automobiles, "America: Love it or Leave it."

Thomas Hooker set a precedent for another use of space to relieve tensions when he voluntarily left Newtown and helped found Connecticut, in order to put more distance between himself and John Cotton with whom he frequently disagreed. Such voluntary escape from uncongenial surroundings fast became and is today part of the American way of life. Does a family have frequent trouble with the neighbors? No matter who is at fault, the family may simply move away in search of more pleasant relationships. Often such moves are made when there has been no trouble, but simply a desire to seek positive associations not found in the old location. Even when employment does not require moving, such changes of residence often occur frequently during a lifetime. Indeed, many Americans do not try to settle down anywhere, choosing rather to live on wheels in a trailer-house.

As we observed earlier, such high mobility weakens the controls exercised by social approval and censure and so tends to increase crime. At the same time, Americans prize their own personal freedom and define it in part as their privilege of living their own lives untrammeled by the opinion of their neighbors. "How we live is none of the neighbors' business" is a typical comment. This common attitude of Americans is at least partly due to the fact that they and their ancestors have for generations been able readily to escape the vicinity of other people. Hence the controls of social custom sit lightly on American shoulders, leaving an impossibly heavy task for the law.

Running Out of Space.

Unclaimed land is now in short supply. There are great areas which bear no houses, it is true. But land sufficiently fertile and otherwise suitable for residence and support is so expensive that few individuals can afford enough to provide for a family. The great majority of Americans are now able to live at or near present standards only by participating in a highly industrialized economy. This means that they must live near the sources of their present livelihood, usually urban.

We are becoming ever more crowded together at home, at work, and on the road. Our custom of doing as we individually please makes us resentful that other people's automobiles and the trucks essential to our commerce and industry cramp our freedom on the highways. At home, the neighbors' loud radios and television sets, unruly children and dogs interfere with our own style of life, while we may be loathe to curb our own activities which annoy our neighbors.

All this, and now the energy shortage! The shortage of gasoline does more than interfere with our going to work or to the shopping centers and home again. *That* problem could be solved by car pools and a wide variety of public transportation. The fuel shortage is the beginning of a threat to our traditional American liberty of individual movement in space by private automobile, whether for an afternoon drive or a cross-country vacation.

Konrad Lorenz, in his best seller *On Aggression,* has made us aware that human beings, like many other creatures, tend to become violently aggressive when overcrowded. In the United States crowding is especially hard to take. American temperaments have developed in conditions permitting the achievement of liberty by the use of space. When our people of radically different traditions and life-styles compete for the limited jobs, housing and elbow-room of our crowded cities, their crowding and frustration lead, with frightful frequency, to the vain escapes offered by alcohol or addictive drugs, or to a violent lashing out against unfortunate victims who happen to be near. The drugs only slightly postpone, then aggravate the problem by requiring additional money. The alcohol often releases inhibited hostilities. Both these attempts to escape, then, actually increase the danger of crime.

Substituting Walls for Space.

Since we no longer have much available space to which criminal offenders or strongly disliked nonconformists can be banished, and we cannot readily move away from them, we now resort to walls. The majority of incarcerated people have given no evidence of being dangerous. But a prison wall, like empty geographical space, serves to put people offensive to us out of our sight.

Imprisonment is not a satisfactory substitute for space. People in prison are a heavy financial burden on taxpaying citizens. Most of them cannot be kept behind walls indefinitely. Life terms for most offenders would be both flagrantly unjust and an insufferable burden on the rest of society. Moreover, prison walls do not separate people from society. They divide society into parts. The more inmates, officials, secretaries, professional staff and security officers are in prisons, the more of society is there. We like to forget this and put the inside of prisons both out of sight and out of mind. We are rudely awakened when prison riots break into the news. Much more frequent shock occurs when people brutalized in prisons come out by escape, completion of their terms, or on parole and put into practice what they have learned "inside."

No longer can we solve our problems of tension between races, peoples of different national origins, or groups with clashing customs, values and life-styles, by moving away from each other. Although I see no way to avoid some locking up of dangerous individuals, it is sheer folly to use separation of prison walls as the normal and usual solution to problems of deviant behavior. Unclaimed space is in short supply and large-scale use of imprisonment is a wretched substitute.

After 200 years, the United States of America now confronts a new requirement, the necessity of living with its social tensions and resolving them right where we are. We have, at this bicentennial period, a rendezvous with destiny. We are called upon by the realities of a settled national area and limited resources to face our problems at home and learn to live with each other. This necessity will demand of us such maturity, rational sobriety, and patience as will be exceedingly difficult to muster. But today there is no way of escape.

11. Contest of the Two Americas

In what direction does the United States intend to go in this, its third century? What will be the primary purpose as it grapples with its problems—whether of energy, housing, medical care, inflation, unemployment, or *crime?* American tradition of national and personal purpose does not speak with one voice. Yet in the vexatious issues concerning the defining of public purpose relative to crime and the criminal, authentic Judaism, Christian theology and our major heritage of secular political philosophy are on the same side.

The problem arises principally from the presence of a strong

American tradition flagrantly contrary to our heritage of great religious and humane secular philosophy. This countertradition has much to do also with the high rate of crime.

There are two Americas. We live in the ever-present context of both and they often affect the thought and action of the same people.

America A: Beautiful Land of Generous Community.

America A is generous, community-minded, benevolent, and humane. All three of our high ethical traditions have contributed to it. Christian teaching emphasizes lovingkindness, fellowship, active concern for the weak and the sacred dignity of every human individual, regardless of his age, ancestry, condition, or moral worthiness. Judaism stresses the justice of opportunity for all, the need to embody concern for the poor in law, the obligation of public benevolence and the responsibility of every individual to serve the community according to his means and ability. From the best political philosophy of our founding fathers, especially Thomas Jefferson, we have drawn the doctrine that "all men are created equal" in political and civil rights. They taught that there should be no discrimination on grounds of religion or race, and that justice and peace should be sought with self-restraint, patience, care for the truth, and generous consideration of others.

America A offers a truly magnificent heritage. It produced the Mayflower Compact, with its pledge of mutual loyalty to the community as a whole. It breathes in the Declaration of Independence based on the "self-evident" truths "that all men are created equal, that they are endowed by their Creator with certain unalienable Rights, that among these are Life, Liberty and the pursuit of Happiness." America A gave us the Bill of Rights, the ten precious constitutional amendments which guarantee our civil liberties. It offers education to all our children. America A has developed popular higher education, and public philanthropy on an unequaled scale. Abraham Lincoln represented it in his pledge and actual policy of "malice toward none" and "charity for all." America A returned the Boxer Indemnity to the Chinese people and showed unprecedented magnanimity toward the Japanese and all of Europe following World War II. It was expressed in the cooperation of our pioneers, sharing the little they had in the face of hardship and in founding of the Red Cross. It appears today in united community funds and in unequaled voluntary support of our religious institutions.

America A is truly "America the Beautiful" and it rightly claims the pride and devotion of all citizens.

America B: Tradition of Aggressive Individualism.

Unfortunately, over against America A stands America B. It is not a mere frequent failure to live up to the high standards of our best utterances and deeds. America B is a tradition deliberately promoting, urging, and glorifying ideas directly contrary to those we have been considering. That they *are* contrary is too seldom recognized.

America B is tightfisted, individualistic, self-righteous, materialistic, aggressive, impatient, vindictive, and prone to violence. In international and interethnic relations, it is quick to resort to arms. Theodore Roosevelt often praised that propensity to violence as a sign and stimulant of American character. In economic affairs it is sometimes called "rugged individualism" and sometimes "the American way."

It began as the colonial immigrants were naturally selected as the more impatient, discontented, and ambitious among their European countrymen. The hard struggle to tame the wilderness and the violent conquest of the Indians strengthened this heritage. Through more than three centuries American pioneers and economic adventurers have been able to gain fabulous riches by hard work, fast aggressiveness, and ruthless disregard for others. Many built their wealth on slave labor. Never, anywhere, have so many people been lured by such great natural resources. Is it surprising that we Americans are known all round the world for our hard-driving, individualistic aggressiveness?

America B is not all bad! Some of its qualities account for much achievement. Impatient discontent with things as they are and a quick readiness to seek actively for better ways can, when well directed, lead to useful inventions, rapid exploration and taming of the wilderness, and to discovery and progress in every sector of life.

Unfortunately, our vaunted tradition of aggressive effort to "get ahead" and "win big," whatever the obstacles, produces other results which are less attractive. America B defended the slave trade in 1776, against Jefferson's attack, and deleted his condemnation of it from the Declaration of Independence. It perpetuated slavery, even at Monticello, and on through the Civil War. In our Puritan past America B defended the *lex talionis* of eye for eye, life for life, drawn from the Old Testament, many centuries after Jesus had denounced it and the Jewish Mishnah had so reinterpreted it as to substitute moderate penalties for vindictive retaliation. In the 1970s the vindictive voices again ring through our legislative halls in the scramble to make political capital of efforts to restore the death penalty.

America B produced massacres of poor straggling remnants of the Indians and has scrapped many Indian treaties. It spawned the Know-Nothing bigots to attack late European immigrants. It urged on the nightriders of the Ku Klux Klan and barbarous lynching parties. Recently America B produced the notorious 1960 conspiracy of the largest manufacturers of electrical goods, the murders at My Lai and the aerial bombing massacres in Southeast Asia—and Watergate.

America B as Seedbed of Crime.

Former President Richard M. Nixon exemplified and expressed especially clearly the ideals of America B. He frequently praised the virtues of people doing things "for themselves" (not for others). Even while accumulating wealth, his benevolent contributions were shockingly paltry. He showed little or no sympathy for people who were unable to support themselves. The Watergate investigations have exposed a circle of conspirators in his Oval Office for whom winning an election was not enough. They must "destroy" the opposition, even if they must use forgery, burglary, misdirection of official agencies, and criminal concealment of evidence for the purpose.

It was precisely the egomania of that Oval Office which led to the automatic taping of all that was said there "for history," and so provided the most decisive evidence bringing about Mr. Nixon's downfall. So strong was his self-righteousness that after publication of the incriminating tapes, his resignation, and admissions of guilt by several staff members, and even as he accepted his successor's pardon, he continued to maintain that he had only made some errors of judgment in his efforts to serve the country. It is no accident that Mr. Nixon and his attorney general, John N. Mitchell, before their public disgrace, had few rivals in demands for harsh treatment of law breakers. Individual aggressiveness, ruthless ambition, self-righteousness, and merciless vindictiveness—all belong together in America B.

Is it any wonder that America B has produced the highest rate of murders and other violent crimes in any developed nation? Competitive advertisers sponsor television shows featuring violence, without regard to the public good. Between scenes of mayhem and gunplay they use every device they can contrive to persuade the viewer that this or that luxury is indispensable to a healthy, successful, sexually attractive life. For millions who are persuaded, there is no lawful way to obtain these things. Many have insufficient sales resistance and America A character to turn aside the appeal to their own America B aggressive ambition. So they get the things they were told they must have, by unlawful means, often violent or threatening violence. Sometimes they take out the anger of their frustration, at some early opportunity, on anyone unlucky enough to cross their paths at the wrong time. Alternatively, they seek escape from their frustration with the help of drugs or alcohol and often crime then becomes a secondary result.

I do not condone the crime. Far from it! I do point out that so

long as so many people with power in the business establishment
and the government actively exemplify and promote the ideals of
America B, the rate of crime at all levels will continue to be excessively high. Individuals with respected positions cannot place
their own selfish interests above the needs of the community and
use dishonest short cuts to gain financial or political advantage and
then reasonably expect the poor and disadvantaged to play by the
rules enacted for the public good.

Organized crime, too, rises naturally from the cultural matrix
of America B. From the unprincipled methods of the "robber
barons," the deliberate overruns of billion-dollar contracts with the
Pentagon, the false advertising of worthless or injurious medicines
and "the game plan" of the Nixon White House to the organized gangsters of the rackets there is only a continuous gradation
of antisocial violence even when there are not direct secret ties.
All alike have made wealth and power the supreme goods and all
obscure moral protests under a haze of deception and smooth
public relations.

Contradictions in Criminal Justice.

The oppositions in American society appear in criminal justice
as well as in other aspects of our national life. If we compare our
practice with that of other advanced democratic countries, we must
conclude that on the whole the vindictive, harsh qualities of
America B dominate our treatment of convicted lawbreakers. But
that is not the whole story.

Occasionally, a defendant appears in court who seems to be
guilty of an offense for which the legally prescribed penalties, dic-
tated by waves of panic and anger, seem unjustly severe. The judge
or jury then finds him "not guilty" rather than subjecting him
to the over-punishment prescribed. Much more frequently the
police do not vigorously pursue such people or the prosecutor does
not arraign them.

When a judge or parole board has wide latitutde, as is usual, some convicted persons are handled with astonishing leniency. Sometimes this is due to corruption. On other occasions it is because something about the offender or the persuasive approach of his lawyer touches a responsive chord in the more benevolent side of the official's disposition. Often it is an aspect of the convicted person which in some way identifies him with the socioeconomic class of the judge or parole board member and so stirs sympathetic understanding.

Such inconsistent workings of the law weaken the positive effect of the criminal justice system. Neither the prisoner who is punished with unusual severity nor the one who "gets off easy" has much respect for the law. Men of both kinds have told me in prison conversations that the law was "just a lottery" or "a game the lawyers play." All this adds up to a significant part of our confused and ineffective "non-system."

New Pressures for Taming America B.

Our high ideals which constitute America A constantly exert pressure on us to reduce the force of America B or at least to curb its excesses. The quantity of violent crime among us should move us further in that direction. Unfortunately, a rise in the crime rate more often calls forth vindictive demands for harsher punishment, strengthens the power of America B among us, and so further increases crime. Serious studies of crime, like those of the President's Commission which reported in 1967 and the National Advisory Commission on Criminal Justice Standards and Goals published in 1973, urge more efficient and more moderate law enforcement, along with more social justice throughout the whole community. Little change has resulted.

Now we are pressed by other forces which may strengthen America A and lead to a higher quality of common life, with similar effects in the system of criminal justice. The rapid expansion in production of *things* demanded by America B ambition is fast driving us into a crisis of limited energy and overburdened ecological life chain. The fast growth of population would be hard enough to sustain. But at the same time, the insatiable demand of the economic system for production and sale of more manufactured goods greatly magnifies the difficulty. The necessary growth could be made in services as well as in goods, but our materialistic ambitions will not permit that. The result is the reckless waste of deliberate obsolescence and innumerable throwaways, from bottles to automobiles.

We shall all soon be compelled to realize, as many now do, that the limited resources of earth require us to change radically our typical American objectives. Possibly, in the process, we shall learn to give higher priority to quality of community life and a lower place to individual, aggressive competition for more material things. Such a change would bring us into a more gentle and benevolent society and a consequent decrease of crime. In such a society we should also predictably change our objectives in criminal justice from so much anger and vindictiveness against past offenders to more concern for aid to victims and prevention of future crime.

At such a time as this we need to ask urgently, What are the goals which ought to guide our national aspirations and our specific programs of official and unofficial action? Our question of basic purpose cannot be answered by America B. The tradition of America B has betrayed us into increasing crime, an ominous depletion and pollution of natural resources and kinds of criminal justice which are destructive, costly, and ineffective. Our question of basic purpose is a question in ethics. For an answer we must look to the more seriously constructed and responsible major ethical traditions of the American people. We are seeking especially goals and norms for criminal justice. We shall see, however, that our great moral traditions have much wider implications, affecting all institutions in the nation.

QUESTIONS FOR THOUGHT

1. How do you interpret the law, "life for life, eye for eye, tooth for tooth" in Exodus 21:23–25? Why do you think the Puritans made it basic in their criminal law despite Jesus' repudiation of it (Matt. 5:38–41)?

2. How would you account for Jefferson's slaveholding, in view of his various published statements severely condemning slavery? Are there parallel contrasts today between public declarations and personal practices?

3. Is there anything which federal or state governments should do today to compensate for broken treaties and other violations of Indian rights?

4. Is there discrimination against people of any particular national origins in your community? If so, what defense is made of such discrimination? What do you think of the matter? If none of the minority groups is represented in your community, would members of them be welcome as residents?

5. Pick a television channel in a period of catering to children and watch it for two hours without changing channels. Take notes on every violent act observed. How many such acts did you see? What effect would the commercials have in a poverty-stricken home with inadequate diet?

6. Can you illustrate the use of space to relieve tensions from your own observation? De facto segregated housing? A church moving from the inner city to escape problems there? A family moving away from uncongenial neighbors? Other?

7. How is America A exemplified in your community? Think of all the other local examples of it you can.

8. What examples of America B have you observed in the past year on the national level? In your state government? In your community or city?

9. What can you do, alone, or with others, to strengthen Amer-
    ica A?

SUGGESTED FURTHER READING

Michael Kammen, *People of Paradox: An Inquiry Concerning the Origins of American Civilization.* Paperback. New York: Vintage Books, 1973.

Ferdinand Lundberg, *The Rich and the Super-Rich.* Paperback. New York: Bantam Books, 1968.

Thomas F. Grossett, *Race: The History of an Idea in America.* Paperback. New York: Schocken Books, 1971.

Richard Hofstadter and Michael Wallace, eds., *American Violence: A Documentary History.* Paperback. New York: Vintage Books, 1971.

PART IV

12. Emerging Agreement on Legal Ethics

We have three major traditions of serious quest for ethical truth in the United States—Jewish, Christian, and secular philosophical. Scholars of each tradition often disagree among themselves and religious ethical teachings also differ from the secular philosophical. What chance do we have of finding a common core of standards for guidance of public policy? Is that not an impossible task?

Actually, on those issues which most concern the system of criminal justice, we shall find a remarkably broad and useful consensus. Not all moral philosophers nor all Christian and Jewish ethicists can be included in such a consensus at every point. Yet there has been a distinct trend of convergence and some ideals embodied in the common teaching have been implanted deeply in the American conscience.

Many Americans try to be faithful to these ideals for whatever reasons their own traditions and thinking provide. Many others do not think much about them, but do readily subscribe to them when they hear or see them expressed and freely acknowledge that they ought to be more faithful to them. I believe that these two classes of people together constitute a large majority of the adult population. If our criminal justice system is to be effective while our civil liberties are maintained, the system must be deeply rooted in

this better American conscience nurtured by the three major
traditions.

Justice Oliver Wendell Holmes said that the law was "the witness and external deposit of our moral life." So it must be if it is to
be effective. At present our criminal law reflects its varied and
confused history. If we are to make it whole and reasonably effective, we shall need to decide what we want with it. That means

principally that we must decide what is truly just—an ethical
question.

Jewish Ethics.

A basic principle of Jewish ethics is *chesed,* the *steadfast love*
attributed to God, but expected also of his people. "You shall love
your neighbor as yourself," in the Hebrew Torah (Lev. 19:18),
originally applied only to fellow Israelites and "the stranger within
the gates." But even as Jesus extended it to include all human beings, so has the Hebrew Midrash extended it to all Gentiles from
ancient times. Lovingkindness, it is taught, does not stand over
against justice, but must enter into it and even, ideally, control it.
So strong is this motif that for many centuries the Jewish scholars
have repudiated retributive punishment. Instead of an eye for an

eye, they teach restitution to the victim and for the offender deterrence, disablement, and rehabilitation.

Respect for the *human dignity* of every person is a second emphatic teaching and is derived from belief that God created all in his own image. Even a person who seems incorrigibly evil still has rights, it is insisted, and they must be respected.

A *community of mutual support* is presupposed in the principle of *chesed*. In the United States today, the rabbis teach a special obligation to all fellow Jews and most rabbis teach also such an obligation to the nation Israel. But they teach benevolence of many kinds in the pluralistic American community.

Guarding the poor and weak from injustice is a special responsibility rooted deeply in the teachings of the Old Testament prophets and Books of Law and elaborated in later writings.

Precise laws publicized in advance of enforcement are strictly required by Jewish teaching and ancient example.

Avoidance of over-burdensome laws is necessary, the Jewish scholars teach in both ancient and modern times. Laws which require what cannot reasonably be expected of the majority are invalid, it is said.

Presumption of innocence until guilt has been established in court is a principle enshrined in our Constitution (Amendments V and VI). The principle goes back to ancient Hebrew law and came to America through English common law.

Strict rules of evidence are prescribed. According to the Mishnah, minors, professional gamblers, and persons under sentence for crime, among others, could not testify in court.

Reinstatement of punished offenders is required. The Mishnah forbids even the mention to a repentant sinner that he did wrong in the past (Bava Matzi'a 4:10).

Restitution to victims of crime was commonly required of offenders in ancient times (Exod. 22:1–17; Lev. 6:1–7) and has been further taught in later centuries.

Christian Ethics.

Law has no such prominence in Christian ethics as in Judaism. The opposition of love to law in the Gospels and of grace to law in the Letters of Paul have even tended to produce an estrangement between Christian ethics and law.

The Roman Catholic church met the issue long ago by setting natural law ethics over human law and adding an ecclesiastical legal order for governance in the church. The counsels of perfection are more exacting than these and guide the members of religious orders in their aspirations to true holiness. The Protestant Reformers rejected this structure of law. They taught that salvation is by grace through faith alone, and that all Christians, not only members of special orders, are called to seek perfection of life by the help of God.

Modern Protestant scholars have rarely had much, if anything, to say about criminal justice. Even more rarely have they tried to give positive definitions or norms of criminal justice. Pope Pius XII and the popular English Protestant lay author C. S. Lewis both defended sheer retribution. But they represented a rear guard action soon to be overtaken by Vatican Council II and other recent expressions of more humane views.

The World Council of Churches sponsored, in 1970, a Consultation on Penal Policies, with over fifty participants from fourteen countries. Prison administrators, social workers, prison chaplains, and lawyers were included, as well as theologians. The members reported agreement that "society itself needs to change," and not solely the offender. They agreed also that "the primary aim of prisons is to help the offender to integrate himself into the community as well as possible on release. It was also widely agreed that present prison systems do not do this," and it was questioned whether they could ever do so. The scope of criminal law needed to be narrowed. Christians were said to be obliged to assist prisoners and ex-prisoners. The purpose of law must not be moral condemnation of persons, but punishment of acts.

In the United States, an Interreligious Task Force on Criminal Justice was established in 1973, representing nearly all the larger Christian churches, some smaller ones and also the Jewish community. The Task Force is mainly directed toward action. However, early in 1974, the members decided to draw up a basic statement of Philosophical and Theological Foundations which would undergird and give ethical guidance to proposals on criminal justice in the United States. A committee of five was appointed to prepare such a statement. I was named chairman and prepared a preliminary proposal. After minor changes and some additions for more explicit clarity, the report was adopted by unanimous vote. That statement is the first for this purpose in the United States.

The principles which the Interreligious Task Force endorsed are in complete accord with the "Agreed Guidelines for Criminal Justice" appearing toward the end of the present chapter and are largely identical in substance. They accord well also with the next two chapters. The fact that they were adopted by a group representing twenty-three bodies—from Friends to Roman Catholics, American Baptists to Unitarians, and Lutherans to Methodists, and Jews as well as Christians—confirms my belief that I am accurately representing an emerging ethical consensus.

These expressions of religious views and concerns regarding criminal justice are impressive as representing the kinds of outlook which informed and responsible Christian clergy and laypersons are reaching when they seriously study the issues together. However, few have engaged in such study and thus far the work of the task force is not widely known.

We must seek authentic Christian teachings affecting the American conscience relative to criminal justice principally in the literature of Christian ethics not dealing explicitly with criminal law.

The New Testament, as well as recent writings, must be cited. Roman Catholics are now seeking guidance directly from the New Testament more often than in many previous centuries. Protestant pastors and lay people are generally influenced more by appeal to the New Testament than by the quoting of scholars or of church agencies.

The Puritans, it is true, depended mainly on a literal and legalistic reading of the Pentateuch, in framing their criminal laws, and gave surprisingly little attention to the stress on mercy and love in the later prophets and the New Testament. Excepting some elements of the extreme conservative movements, most American Christians now acknowledge a superior claim for the teachings of Jesus. Most present-day Christians will, I believe, recognize the principles below as authoritative for the Christian conscience.

Love and respect for all persons are nearly always acknowledged as the first principles properly governing the relations of human beings. Jesus designated the commandments to love God and neighbor as the two greatest and added, "On these two commandments depend all the law and the prophets" (Matt. 22:37–40). He made it clear that every person is to be treated as a neighbor (Luke 10:29–37). The church has traditionally followed Paul in making love the supreme virtue (1 Cor. 13:13). In contemporary ethical writing, Christian scholars as different as Paul Ramsey, Joseph Fletcher, and Charles E. Curran, put love in the supreme place.

Two men have recently touched the American conscience especially deeply by appeal to the spirit of Christian love. Pope John XXIII, in his last encyclical, said, "May Christ inflame the desires of all men to break through the barriers which divide them, to strengthen the bonds of mutual love, to learn to understand one another, and to pardon those who have done them wrong." Martin Luther King, Jr., constantly stressed love as central. He said truly, in the preface of *Stride Toward Freedom,* that the book was "the chronicle of 50,000 Negroes"—in Montgomery—"who learned to fight for their rights with the weapon of love."

Love in the New Testament sense always includes respect for the human dignity of the other person. Without such respect there may be lust or other kinds of personal attraction or exploitation, but not love.

Seeking to nurture and maintain community is a closely related requirement of New Testament ethics. The church was born in an outpouring of God's Spirit, binding together believers who gladly shared food, possessions, homes, teachings, praise to God, and joy (Acts 2). In the Gospel of John, Jesus is represented as praying repeatedly for his disciples and all future followers "that they may all be one; even as thou, Father, art in me, and I in thee" (John 17:21). Writers on Christian ethics generally agree that this fellowship (*koinonia*) ought to share as generously and fully as possible with all people.

Due *humility and restraint* must be exercised in rendering judgments. We have no right to judge the real moral responsibility of other persons (Matt. 7:1). God alone knows the secrets of the heart and he is the one true judge of our motives and intentions (Heb. 4:12–13). Nevertheless, Christian churchmen have often been self-righteous and censorious. In recent decades there has been a strong reaction against such pride in both Roman Catholic and Protestant circles.

Special care for the poor and weak has a long history in the Christian churches. Christians have turned, increasingly, in this century, to expressing their caring in social policy as well as in individual relief.

Forgiveness and mercy are stressed wherever Christians repeat, in the Lord's Prayer, "Forgive us our trespasses as we forgive those who trespass against us." Christians everywhere read and hear the story of Jesus' refusal to condemn the woman taken in adultery, even while he did condemn the act when he said, "Neither do I condemn you; go, and do not sin again" (John 8:11).

Community of responsibility for sin and righteousness, emphatically taught in traditional Christian doctrine, challenges typically individualistic American tendencies. Original sin and the Fall are interpreted differently by various theological schools of thought. Yet they see alike that all of us are bound together in a community of sin. As all have sinned, so all are called now to enter a community of righteousness.

Law is for persons, not persons for law. When a law is put into operation, it tends to develop a kind of independent existence of its own. Many laws remain on the books for years, and even generations, after the occasion has passed which made them useful or which once made legislators think they would be useful. In the New Testament, laws are recognized as necessary, but as becoming harmful when rigidly applied, without adequate regard for persons affected (Mark 2:27; Luke 6:6–10). Law cannot create new, good life, as can lovingkindness. We should have learned to place less reliance on criminal law and more on community-building works of faith and love.

American Secular Ethics.

Within the limits of this small book we cannot survey a wide range of philosophies. We will briefly mention some guiding principles which such a study has shown to be widely supported in different works of philosophical ethics and which are relevant to criminal law and procedure.

Consistency and *coherence with empirical data* are commended by such varied philosophical moralists as John Dewey, Brand Blanshard, Peter A. Bertocci, William K. Frankena, Richard M. Millard, and nearly all others. The same writers see *respect for all persons* as an ethical obligation. In support of it also are such philosophical anthropologists as May and Abraham Edel and the philosophical sociologist Pitirim A. Sorokin, as well as philosophers Gregory Vlastos and William Ernest Hocking.

When our founding fathers declared that "all men are created equal," they were committing the institutions of this nation to the principle of *equality* in basic human rights. They conveniently side-stepped slavery and were probably not aware of the inequities suffered by women, but they saw the principle and stated it unequivocally. Alan Gewirth, Paul A. Freund, and Frankena are among recent philosophers elaborating on this principle. From the obligation to respect all persons ethicists infer the obligation of governments to *interfere minimally with personal freedom*. Vlastos, Frankena, and others have contended that governments are good only as they contribute to good lives. Goodness in a human life implies good will and hence free decision. Government must limit the freedom of decision as little as possible and only to protect the rights of others.

The whole *community* is *responsible* for *opportunities of all persons* and all are responsible for maintaining such a responsible community. Many philosophers have so declared. Bertocci, Millard, Blanshard, Sorokin, Dewey, and the Edels are among them. Freund is especially emphatic in urging that justice to individuals cannot be separated from social justice.

Agreed Guidelines for Criminal Justice.

From this quick survey of converging relevant teachings from the three great ethical traditions in the United States we can now see that a number of ethical norms would have support from all three. If a philosophy of criminal justice and specific laws, sentences, or policies are to be acceptable to the American conscience they must be in accord with these norms.

1. *Consistency and coherence with realities.*

Although philosophical ethics alone has laid much stress on this, it is implicit in the other traditions also. A commitment which one feels free to contradict in the next breath or in practice or in the predictable results of one's practice is not serious. When legislatures or judges act in mere response to waves of emotion, without rational consideration of purposes which the facts indicate can be furthered by the action, as happens frequently, this basic norm is violated.

2. *Benevolent good will and respect for all persons.*

This norm and the requirement of consistent practice form the basis of all others. *A consistent, hence dependable, respectful, benevolent good will toward all persons is the fundamental requirement of ethically defensible criminal justice.*

3. *Equal rights for all persons.*

As far as the law is concerned, this norm is enshrined in Amendment XIV of the Constitution and is supported by the teachings of all our major moral traditions. Yet it is especially far from our practice of criminal justice.

4. *Presumption of innocence.*

The written and oral Torah establish strict safeguards of this principle. The Christian teachings against judgmental attitudes and for love and respect give strong support, as do the Golden Rule and similar formulas of both religious and secular traditions. The presumption of innocence until guilt is proved beyond reasonable doubt is implicit in the Constitution, as strongly affirmed by the Supreme Court, especially in the decision *In Re Winship* (1970).

5. *Special care to protect the poor, weak, and unpopular from unfair treatment.*

Experience shows that without special effort to safeguard such persons, they will be treated unfairly. If we compare the treatment of Mr. Nixon or Mr. Agnew with official actions against countless poor, ignorant, or unpopular defendants every day, we see how important this norm is. Equal rights are mocked by such realities.

6. *Restoration of community when disrupted.*

Both Christian and Jewish ethics stress the importance of community and the obligation of all to sustain and serve it. When it is disrupted by crime, the need for concerned restoration by its members is acute.

7. *Responsibility of all individuals for the community.*

The order of the community is too important and too complex to be left to officials. All citizens share responsibility for the health of the community in proportion to their ability to influence it. Justice is everybody's business.

These guidelines will be helpful as we seek to learn what Americans should do about crime. However, it remains for us to draw our thoughts together in a single vision of true criminal justice, before we try to plan specific changes in law and policy.

13. A Philosophy of Interests

Justice as Fairness.

John Rawls has recently written a book about justice which is much discussed among students of ethics and political philosophy. "What is justice?" he asks, and replies, "Justice is fairness."

Who could object to that? If legislation or a court decision or the treatment of any person was admitted to be unfair, would anyone think it was just? On the other hand, if it was fair could it be unjust?

About now you may object that Rawls's definition has only given us the word "fairness" for the word "justice," without throwing any light on the nature of it. But we would not be fair (or just!) to Rawls if we stopped here. For he goes on to tell how we can test for fairness.

Before we go further, we must explain that he is not writing specifically about criminal justice, but about justice in general, in a whole society. However, as he maintains, if we can get a clear understanding of justice in general, it will then be easier to understand the nature of justice in any particular aspect or agency of society.

What, then, is justice as fairness? That, Rawls argues, is the kind of arrangement which a rational person making a free choice for his own good would choose if he expected to live in the society but had no idea what place he would occupy in it—young or old; smart or dull; executive or laborer; judge or defendant; man or woman.

Now what are the general principles of a just society, that is, principles which rational people would choose "under a veil of ignorance" about the role they were to have? Of course this question can be answered only by exercise of imagination. Why not exercise yours, then? Imagine that you are setting up the government and economy of a new society, without knowing what place you will have in it. As you imagine this, see what you think of Rawls's "first principle": "Each person is to have an equal right to the most extensive total system of equal basic liberties compatible with a similar system of liberty for all" (*A Theory of Justice* [Cambridge, Mass.: Harvard Univ. Press, 1971], p. 302).

If this idea were adopted it would require that we reduce substantially the present scope of American criminal law. We could treat as crimes only such acts as interfered with other people's freedom and for this purpose we could interfere with the offenders' freedom only so far as necessary to protect the freedom of others.

We are not discussing here Rawls's other principles nor the elaborate discussion of his 600 pages. We pause only to notice that his second principle requires a fair (not equal) distribution of economic and social goods and equal opportunity to gain the various desirable positions.

For our interest in criminal justice, we turn now to the foremost legal philosopher the United States has produced, Roscoe Pound (1870–1964).

Justice as Balancing Interests.

Justice, thought Pound, is a balancing of individual, social, and public interests. The relations between the social and public interests are ambiguous and at times Pound drops the class of public interests, as we will do.

Individual interests include such individual rights as freedom of the person from threats, assaults, or pressures; honor and reputation from wanton insult or defamation; belief, opinion, and free speech against needless restraint. Included also are domestic relations and various economic rights.

Social interests include interests of the state against treason, interference with the machinery of government and foreign invasion, also the security of such social institutions as family, church, political and economic structures, the general morals, natural resources, and opportunity for individuals to develop. Social interests, then, concern the social arrangements which are of concern to a number of individuals or even to all in the society.

It soon becomes obvious that certain arrangements or experiences which some persons are interested in having are not worthy of being served or protected. Some individuals demand the right to defraud the poor and gullible, others to spread heroin addiction among youth for their own profit. Justice does not require defending interests of certain persons in activities which damage the harmless or socially useful interests of others. Justice is a balanced serving of those interests which can be joined harmoniously in a whole personal and social life. As Pound says, "Secure all interests so far as possible with the least sacrifice of the totality of interests or the scheme of interests as a whole" (*Jurisprudence* [St. Paul: West Publ. Co., 1959], vol. 3, pp. 342–343).

Justice as Love Equitably Distributed.

Are not both Rawls's and Pound's main principles precisely the ones required by lovingkindness as supported by all our great ethical traditions?

Rawls's theory of justice as fairness might be regarded as an elaborate and imaginative way of stating the Golden Rule in a situation where complex interests of many others must be considered. If I am planning—or judging and reforming—a government or any agency of government and want to do to others as I would want them to do to me, what others should I consider? Why, *all,* of course, who will be affected. Does not this require my imaginatively putting myself in all the various roles, as Rawls advocates?

In the courtroom various opposing interests are represented. How will the judge follow the Golden Rule there? To put it another way, how will he act in lovingkindness, or in benevolent respect for every person to be affected by his judgment? Clearly, he must consider not only the people in the courtroom, but also other people in the community who will be affected by his decision. If he is a man of benevolent lovingkindness toward all persons, will he not have to do the best he can to balance all these various interests and do what, in the long run and on the whole, will be best for all concerned?

Chief Justice Stanley E. Qua of the Massachusetts Supreme Judicial Court once had an extended conversation with me in his chambers on my question, What is a just disposition of a criminal case when the defendant has been found guilty. In reply, he first discussed limits put on his action by the laws. Then he pointed out that the convicted person before the bar has certain interests which the judge must consider. But so also he must consider the victim of the criminal act, the families and friends of both, and even the whole neighborhood disturbed by the crime. Even more! He must consider the structure of the law itself and the need of all the people in the community to have the law respected for the sake of their secure, orderly life. This did not mean that the offender would count for very little, as only one among so many. For if there is to be a sentence, it will affect him more than anyone else. The judge must therefore take him into serious account, along with all the others.

Lovingkindness in the courtroom is no simple matter! Justice is both a serious and a complex business. It is also obviously a fine art and not an exact science.

If we accept the idea that justice is lovingkindness or benevolence distributed what should be the central meaning and purpose of criminal justice? Retribution? Deterrence? Disablement? Rehabilitation? We must see now whether we can bring our understanding of justice into a more inclusive and definite focus.

14. Justice as Social Defense and Social Restoration

Retribution Rejected.

"An eye for eye" cannot in any way be defended, if justice is judged by the serving of individual and community interests. An effort to balance moral guilt for a past deed by inflicting present or future discomfort for the sake of the balancing itself is obviously not intended to serve any person's or community's interests. If punishment is designed to serve an interest in defense against future crime, then the purpose is not retribution, but disablement, deterrence, rehabilitation, or some other forward-looking goal.

Proper Place for Deterrence and Disablement.

The community has the right—yes, and the *duty*—to protect all its individual members from crime. In this task, deterrence has its place, as we observed earlier, especially in protecting against the more rational, cool-headed crimes, such as embezzlement, violations of housing codes, fraud and other white collar crimes. When a *moderate* penalty is put into effect *soon* and *surely* after a crime it may have considerable deterrent effect against a wider variety of crimes, although less than popular opinion supposes. Within limits, then, deterrence is a valid consideration of justice.

Disablement or incapacitation also passes the tests of our ethical guidelines and if it stops the criminal activities of an offender

without doing too much injury to him or his family, it will even serve his best interests in the long run. Certainly it often serves the interest of the community of citizens.

Rehabilitation.

Valid interests of both offender and community are served when the convicted offender is returned to freedom prepared to live as a law-abiding and useful citizen. Efforts to accomplish this by various programs in our prisons are usually disappointing in results. The persons whose interest in staying out of trouble has been assisted to fulfillment should be grateful for such help. So should the rest of the community. But we all have reason to wish this were accomplished more regularly.

There are two evident causes for the proportion of disappointments. The first is the inherently dehumanizing and destructive nature of imprisonment. At best, it is difficult to teach responsibility in free decisionmaking in a place where the inmate has few decisions to make, bears little responsibility and is being told by the very walls around him that he is not trusted and is not free. Actual conditions in most prisons add far more indignities and evil influences. The second cause defeating a large proportion of efforts to rehabilitate is that these efforts are focused on the individual in isolation from family and other people for whom he might care.

The principal roots of crime are in the home and neighborhood. If crime is to be significantly reduced it must be done there. All the national commissions which have made serious studies of crime in recent years have emphasized this truth.

Social Defense and Restoration.

A person who feels a sense of unity or common concern with the persons around him does not rob, rape, kill, or otherwise intentionally injure them. Since he is concerned for their well-being, he does not even steal from them, whether by passing bad checks, embezzlement, purse snatching, or burglarizing the house in their absence. Crime is itself a symptom of the criminal's alienation or estrangement from other people.

Sometimes the alienation is a purely individual affair. A boy feels unloved, neglected, or unpopular. He becomes, at least in his own feeling, a loner. He may be so everywhere or he may feel alone against the world only at school or on the street.

On the other hand, the alienation may be a group experience. The black people of a community may feel excluded from the mainstream of community life—economic, political, religious, and social. A small group of boys who cannot cope with the assigned studies in school, or whose interests so strongly conflict with the school program that they simply opt out of it, draw together against the rest of their classmates and their teachers.

Either individual or group alienation is a condition favorable to crime. An act of crime further aggravates the division. The person or persons doing the deed increase their own feeling of separation from others. At the same time, the victim or victims are likely to be made angry, suspicious, and afraid. In short, they are at least somewhat alienated too. This may be a reason why people recently *victims* of crime especially often *commit* crime.

When the community is strong in its sense of common concern the crime rate is low. It is also a much happier community than is one divided by cross-currents of hostility and chasms of cold indifference.

Evidence that strong ties of community reduce crime may be seen by looking at small areas of concentrated Chinese population in the midst of our inner cities. With especially high rates of crime all around them, the Chinese exhibit low rates of crime. If you ask the citizens of such a Chinatown why there is so little crime among them, they reply by talking of their strong family ties, their mutual pride and supportive relationships. The individual wants to avoid staining the honor of his larger family. Recently Chinese elders have complained that some of the young people, under the influence of their American friends, were losing their sense of pride in family and community. Consequently, the crime rates in some Chinese neighborhoods have been rapidly rising, of late.

Many other examples, both positive and negative, could be given. We would then include the low rate of crime in African villages living in traditional close community, as contrasted with rapid rises in crime among the many who move as individuals or as immediate ("nuclear") families into the cities where ties with the larger families and village structures are broken.

To prevent crime, then, an especially important goal must be to strengthen ties of community, taking care that no group or individual is excluded. Likewise, when crime has been committed, the purpose of criminal justice must be to mend the alienation which formed the root cause of the crime and particularly to mend the further damage done to community by the crime itself.

In short, what Americans should do about crime, while including many things yet to be specified, must be especially to *strengthen and defend the community continuously, and after a crime to restore its wholeness, with special concern for the persons most affected.* This is what we mean by *social defense and restoration.*

This goal would go far beyond that of *reintegration* now advocated by many criminologists. The goal of reintegrating the offender into society is certainly far more realistic and helpful than the usual model of rehabilitation which focuses only on the offender as an individual. Reintegration would assist him into old or new roles in his family, peer group, and neighborhood. Such goals of rehabilitation as self-control, responsibility, work habits, and character are nearly meaningless and certainly unachieveable apart from relations with other people. The integrationists see this clearly and so would cultivate such relations as will make possible a future law-abiding life in the community. This goal requires cultivation of the offender's relationships in the community where he is to live.

Social defense and restoration agrees with reintegration but goes far beyond it. Not only does the individual offender need to change relationships with other people. The family, neighborhood, and larger community also need change. To reintegrate an individual into a disordered, alienated, or violence-prone family or neighborhood is not good enough. The crime was a symptom of a fracture in community relationships. The criminal act has further disrupted the fabric of community. Criminal justice must address the brokenness of this social network and not only that of the individual offender's character and of his own social relations.

How would that work? Look at a relatively simple situation where it *does* work. Then we will suggest ways of moving in the same direction in our complex urban life.

Among the Shona-speaking people in traditional villages of Rhodesia—or Zimbabwe as they prefer to call it—community life is very close. Many activities are done together—like building a house, digging a well, or herding the cattle. Morning greetings always include detailed inquiries about the other's health and the members of his family. When Josiah congratulates Abel on a recent success, Abel replies (in approximate translation), "It's all of us." Congratulations on the birth of a baby or on a marriage bring similar responses. This is not mere formality. It expresses a deep feeling of belonging together as one people diminished or augmented by the joys or sorrows, achievements or disgraces of each individual.

When a man in such a village steals, assaults, or otherwise injures another, the subchief or headman must first find out who committed the crime. After that, his attention is directed to working out a plan for restitution, as well as possible, to the victim, victims, or next of kin. Eventually the offender and his family must give to the headman part or all the food for a community feast to celebrate the conclusion of the affair. The victim(s) will have received cattle, money, or labor from the offender and his family. At the high point of the feast, the headman will recount to all what has been done. Then he will ask the victim and family, "Are you satisfied?" They will reply that they are satisfied. Then he will ask the offender and his family whether they are satisfied. They, too, will reply affirmatively. The headman will ask all assembled whether they are satisfied. After their affirmative reply, he will solemnly intone, "Then it is finished." After that the community is whole again and it would be intolerably ill-mannered for anyone ever to mention again the crime that was done.

We cannot accomplish similar goals in the same way here in

our complex and already deeply fragmented society. But what could we do to move in the direction of such social defense and restoration?

We will start by observing some things we should do to fortify the community against crime.

QUESTIONS FOR THOUGHT

1. Have you observed a difference between beliefs of church people, Jews, and other persons concerning criminal justice in your community?

2. Do the ethical guidelines at the end of Chapter 12 agree with your own moral convictions?

3. When you watch a judge sentencing a convicted lawbreaker, does he appear to be trying to do the best he can for all concerned? To be indifferently handing down the sentence in routine fashion? To be expressing the anger of the community against the offender? Do you see signs of other motives or purposes?

4. Do you agree with the author's rejection of retribution? Can a judge know the measure of the moral responsibility of an offender? Is there a way of determining how many days —months—years of incarceration would be equal to his or her moral guilt? Has your answer implied a purpose different from retribution, such as deterrence or disablement?

5. What cases of white-collar crime do you know? Have the culprits received sentences roughly equivalent to those given poor people who stole similar amounts or did similar damage to public order?

6. What efforts are made in the jail or prison nearest you to turn inmates to a useful and law-abiding life? Are other such efforts made in your city, county, or state through correctional personnel in the field, as probation and parole officers? What proportion of people who come out on parole in your community are convicted of new crimes? Do many citizens try to help them go straight?

7. Are relatives and friends welcome as visitors at the jail or prison nearest you? Do clergymen or concerned lay people visit regularly and offer help?

8. What responsibility do the people of your community feel
   for reducing crime and the conditions which nurture it? Do
   they leave it to the police and other officials?

SUGGESTED FURTHER READING

Struggle for Justice. A Report on Crime and Punishment in America.
Prepared for the American Friends Service Committee. New
York: Hill and Wang, 1971.

Engage/Social Action: Special issues on prisons and criminal justice,
February 1972, August 1973, and June 1975.

L. Harold DeWolf, *Responsible Freedom.* New York: Harper &
Row, 1971.

PART V

HOW AMERICANS SHOULD DEAL WITH CRIME

■

15. Fortifying the Community

The most important things Americans can and ought to do to reduce crime are steps to build and fortify a strong, cohesive, inclusive community. Such actions are mostly outside the formal institutions of criminal justice. But if we take seriously the task of social defense we must look first of all to the strength and soundness of the society we propose to defend. Even when a nation seeks to defend itself against external foes, it must give careful attention to its internal health. How much more is this true when we are concerned with defending against the internal enemy crime, which rises in our own streets and households!

Social Justice.

The President's Commission on Law Enforcement and Administration of Justice reported in 1967 that it had "no doubt whatever that the most significant action that can be taken against crime is action designed to eliminate slums and ghettos, to improve education, to provide jobs, to make sure that every American is given the opportunities and the freedom that will enable him to assume his responsibilities" (*Challenge of Crime,* p. 15). Six years later, in 1973, the National Advisory Commission on Criminal Justice

Standards and Goals said, "The connection between alienation and violence" had been "documented" (*Community Crime Prevention,* p. 3), and devoted a large volume of its official report to urgently needed social reforms. Yet from 1967 on into 1975, the richest Americans continued to get richer and the poor, in every year, remained at about the same level or became poorer. Inflation and high rates of unemployment in 1975 have struck especially hard at the young adult members of minorities. It is not surprising that the Index crimes have continued to increase.

If we truly care for fairness and the "unalienable rights" to which we were committed at our nation's birth, we will give to social justice our highest national priority. American policy already discloses the assumption that we will not allow people in this country to starve. However, we have, for relief or prevention of dire poverty, a confused network of different programs which overlap at some points, miss some people altogether and involve a huge, costly bureaucracy. Some results of spotty planning at different times and for different purposes are socially undesirable. Certain people who have never earned a living, although capable of doing so, receive more money than others with families who work hard and earn near the bottom of the wage scale. In other cases the government is seen as paying women to have illegitimate children and it rewards some young couples for living together without marriage. Meanwhile, investigators heap indignities on the worthy poor. The whole maze of programs for relief of poverty needs thorough overhauling.

The most promising direction to take would appear to be an inclusive form of guaranteed annual income in the form of a negative income tax. As usually proposed, such a program would include automatic incentives for recipients to earn as much as possible of their own support, since every dollar earned would improve their income while also relieving, by a sliding scale, the payment from the government.

Employment and Recreation for Youth.

Hundreds of young men and women roam the streets of our inner cities with no employment available. Hundreds of teenagers also roam about looking for some kind of exciting activity. While this condition exists among the very groups who contribute most heavily to street crimes, such crimes will continue in tragically great volume.

"An ounce of prevention is worth a pound of cure." How true this is concerning crime! Some of the billions now lost to citizens by crime and the cost of fighting crime would be well spent in funding employment when jobs in the private sector are not available. Some young adults—perhaps unemployed school teachers trained in physical education—could be publicly hired to operate recreational programs. Such programs would be investments in countless human lives, affecting a long future.

Design for Crime Prevention.

New York City has found a change in the design of parking meters effective in preventing heavy losses to slug-users, while threats and prosecutions accomplished little. Many cities, troubled by robbery and murder of bus drivers have brought such crimes almost to an end when they have installed locked cash boxes and a no-change policy. Taxicab companies have had a similar experience. Such policies are a small nuisance to the public, but well worth that cost. Adequate lighting of streets and alleys, campaigns to have stores and residences more securely locked, and automatic shoplifting alarm equipment triggered by magnetic tags on articles of clothing being carried near an exit—all these devices have helped reduce crime by making it more difficult. Will not clever professional criminals find ways to overcome such obstacles? Yes, some of them, sometimes. But if you only prevent the first or second crime of a beginner or the one-time impulse of an ordinarily law-abiding person, that will bring great benefits.

For the same reason motorists ought to take their ignition keys and lock the doors when leaving their cars. A professional car thief can gain entrance and start the motors of many locked cars, it is true. But police report that a substantial proportion of cars which are stolen have been left open with the keys in the ignition. This careless practice tempts many a youth to take his first unlawful joyride and may lead to further criminal acts.

Root Out Political Corruption.

Criminals are often released without serving sentence or given only a slap on the wrist for serious crime. In many cases this is due to outright bribery or political contributions to key officials, especially in the prosecutor's office or the parole board. Is it any wonder

that crime flourishes on the street when so many crimes have been
exposed at the highest state and national levels?

Bribery must be vigorously ferreted out and prosecuted, of
course. But political contributions often have similar effect. Contributions to campaigns are the lifeblood of elected legislators and
officials. It takes more and more money to run for office successfully. It takes a person of superior integrity to receive large cam-
paign contributions and then disregard completely appeals made
by the friendly givers in behalf of themselves or others.

Our best aids in cutting down these evils are an alert, investigative press and legislation limiting closely amounts of single contributions, requiring published complete records and, in the case of
state and national elections, providing mostly public funding.

Reduce Violence in the Media.

Television shows specializing in violence have risen, in twenty
years, from 20% to 60% of prime time offerings and in March
1975, twenty-four crime series were on the airwaves (*Newsweek,*
March 10, 1975, p. 81). Defenders of such shows claim that they
do not influence the conduct of viewers, even young ones. If they
don't, then the television companies are badly defrauding American business by charging advertisers thousands of dollars per
minute. Research has shown that television viewing does influence
viewers in different ways. Influenced most are children in homes
with parents poor and ill-educated—precisely the homes from
which come the most juvenile delinquents headed for street crime.
Whether "goodies" or "baddies" win makes little difference. Either
way it is taught that violence is the way to solve problems. Even
children who are not more inclined to commit violent acts after
viewing such scenes on television are found to accept violence as to
be expected and to be less inclined to do anything about it when
they witness violence on the street.

The proposal to restrict the most horrible violence to hours after ten at night would not solve the problem. Not only are many adults vulnerable, but millions of young children, to say nothing of teenagers, especially in poor homes, watch long after ten.

In both movies and television, the cartoons may seem harmless. Actually, one of the most frequent cartoon themes is that the happiest outcome of a problem is violent revenge.

The newspapers, too, by lurid overreporting of sordid details in daily episodes of sexual crimes and violent crimes increase the social atmosphere of endemic violence.

Develop a Caring Community.

When you take food to a sick neighbor, exchange baby-sitting favors or form a car pool, you are increasing the positive bonds of community and helping to fortify it against crime. When men join in painting a church or cleaning up a piece of neglected public land they may not think they are fighting crime, but they are doing so. So is a teen-age boy who draws a loner into a friendly game. Even backfence talk is a help, unless it takes the form of ugly hostility against other neighbors—perhaps a poor family or members of a minority. Close, cooperative, and inclusive community must be the watchword.

A caring kind of community action moves closer to direct relation to crime when it concerns victims of criminal attack. This opens such a neglected and important aspect of criminal justice itself that we will devote the next chapter to it.

16. The Victim—Forgotten Person of American Criminal Justice

If our much-publicized American concern about crime is more than self-centered fear and vindictive anger, then there must be increasing evidence of public interest in victims. We direct the spotlight of attention on the perpetrators of crime. Legislatures and courts debate the civil rights of criminals, the penalties they should suffer, the therapeutic treatments they should receive and the institutions in which they are to live. When a criminal trial and sentencing are finished the convicted person is led away and, usually against his will, supported by the public for a period. The victim, who may be maimed or otherwise injured, has probably lost several days of work to be on hand to testify for the public. Now he walks out, if able to do so, the forgotten person. His career may be ruined, his confidence shattered, his savings

exhausted. Even if a part of the penalty assessed against the offender is a fine, that goes to the public treasury, and with rare exceptions none of it goes to the injured victim.

Who is the Victim?

In Philadelphia, a study discovered, non-white men were twice as likely to be stabbed and over five times as likely to be shot as whites. Blacks also had their pockets picked more than twice as often and were robbed more frequently. Similar facts were found in Chicago. Women were included in the Chicago study and it was found that per 100,000 nearly four times as many non-white women as white women were forcibly raped. If we were to include serious victimization by fraudulent merchandising, we should probably find both blacks and the poor particularly disproportionate among the victims, because of lower average educational levels, more limited legitimate financial credit, and less likely legal prosecution.

Most victims of murder are relatives or associates of the persons killing them. Killings within the family make up nearly one-third of all murders. Especially frequent victims of violent crime are the intoxicated. Greedy gamblers, the well-to-do but unalert elderly and people of careless habits are frequent victims of some kinds of crime. Finally, people who commit crimes are especially often victims. Sometimes a criminal is beaten, robbed, or executed by criminal confederates or competitors. He is also especially vulnerable to blackmail and often a relatively safe object of criminal attention because he dare not call the police.

Responsibility of the Victim.

Some victims bear considerable responsibility for the crimes against them. Often people who are viciously assaulted, even killed, have initiated fights or by harassment have fomented attack. In many cases an aggravated assault or murder is the culmination of a quarrel in which the ultimate victim was until then the more aggressive person.

Sometimes the victim has half intended or fully intended that the crime be committed. This is probably true in a few cases of rape. It is certainly true in some cases of automobile theft and some of arson, when the property owner unable to sell his property desires to collect insurance and so leaves the car keys in the ignition or a house unlocked with paper and matches handy.

Compensation of Victims Elsewhere.

Restitution to victims by persons who have stolen, damaged, or destroyed their property was in former times a requirement of criminal law throughout most of the world, but it is not so now in most developed countries and not in the United States.

As we saw earlier, in much African traditional law, compensation to the victim and the victim's family is the first consideration. That is likewise true in many other societies which we, in our pride, call primitive. There were similar arrangements in Europe until, in the Middle Ages, the Church and state took as fines larger and larger proportions of the payments, finally leaving nothing for the victims. In several European countries payments of compensation have been revived in recent years.

Neglect in American Criminal Law.

Only eight states make any provision to compensate victims of crime. Even in those states such laws come into use relatively seldom, and when they do the compensation is inadequate. In forty-two states there is no such provision at all.

Why is this? One explanation is that people are theoretically free to seek damages by suing persons who have injured them or their interests. The theory is that the state prosecutes a criminal case in behalf of society as a whole, to maintain public order. For wrong suffered by an individual the proper course for him is a private lawsuit. So goes the theory, and occasionally it works—but not often.

The victim, more often than not, lacks the money to engage counsel and file suit. If he can overcome that obstacle, he will probably spend his time and money in vain. Whatever the court may order the offender to pay, it will not be paid. Most people prosecuted under criminal law are poor. If an offender is convicted, his earning power will be further reduced. If he is imprisoned he can earn nothing of consequence because wages paid for work in American prisons run at such token levels as twenty-five cents to one dollar a day.

A second cause for neglect of victims in our laws is that the majority of victims are from segments of the population for whom legislators have little feeling beyond a distant pity.

A third explanation is that even without special knowledge many readers about crime suspect that the victims are partly responsible for the crimes against them. Sometimes they are, as we have observed. It is all too comforting to assume that usually they are. Such an assumption supports both the feeling that "it will never happen to me" and the sense of proud aloofness with which we keep from getting involved.

A fourth reason for our neglect of victims is that we fear the rise in taxes which might be needed to pay for compensation of the many victims in whose behalf no collection could be made from the offenders.

Why Victims Should be Compensated.

Justice, in any situation, requires doing the best possible for all the persons affected. To ignore the victim of a crime violates all the major ethical traditions of our people. It was precisely the care for a victim of crime which Jesus used to illustrate the scope of love in the parable of the good Samaritan. Modern Jewish teaching extends the principles of *chesed* and neighbor love to all members of the community. The humane secular tradition of benevolent ethics would likewise, if consistently applied, require caring for the victims of crime. When the issue is raised, most Americans recognize that basic human decency requires special assistance to victims.

Another reason why we should provide for assistance to victims of crime is the effect of our neglect on the social climate. When victims are left to bear their injuries alone, resentment and bitterness spread in innumerable circles throughout the population. Feeling resentful and frustrated, victims and their friends add to the irrational angers and hatreds which clamor for vindictive retribution and add to the climate favorable to violent crime as well.

If victims were regularly compensated for their injuries there would be an improvement in reporting to the police. Compensation laws usually require such reporting when possible, as they should. Victims would then have an incentive to report, at least offsetting the nuisance of police questioning and possible embarrassment, harassment, danger, and loss of time in court appearances.

Most of all, we should compensate victims of crime because it is just and right. It is ironical and disgraceful that we take and use the angry and vindictive side of venerated custom, while the ancient requirements of lovingkindness our law has, with a few recent exceptions, omitted, even as they apply to the victim who should most readily win our sympathetic and active concern.

How Victims Should be Compensated.

When it is practicable, the offender ought to be required to make direct or indirect restitution. Better still, concerned people may persuade the offender to offer restitution before trial. Often, in a suburban or rural neighborhood, a judge has continued a juvenile case or a prosecutor has delayed the prosecution while youthful offenders have made repairs, paid financial compensation from their own earnings, or "worked off" obligations incurred by vandalism, pilfering, or other delinquent acts. When this has been done, the matter has been officially dropped. Such arrangements sometimes cement positive, friendly relationships between erstwhile victims and young offenders. Sometimes youth administrations make similar arrangements at later stages. They should be used much more often at any stage, usually the earlier the better.

In cases of adults and of older youth involved in the more serious crimes, the problem of making restitution is more difficult. For a crime of violence there is often no possible compensation which is adequate. What price shall be put on a person's life or eyesight or the ability to walk?

How shall an offender pay if he has never even supported himself by honest labor? If he is sentenced to a prison where he cannot earn significant wages, how can he provide even moderate restitution to a person or family to whom he has done injury?

Probation and early parole are being used for ever larger proportions of offenders. Both in Hawaii and in New York, restitution is often made a condition of probation and regular payments are required as a condition of continuing on probation until a prescribed sum has been paid. Work release from prison enables inmates to earn at going rates outside and so makes restitution possible. In a few institutions, industrial contracts filled inside the walls provide for payment at or near prevailing wage levels. More of such arrangements should be made. Restitution should then be required in suitable cases.

Even when restitution by offenders is made in all possible cases, many victims will receive nothing from that source. It must be remembered that even of crimes reported only one out of four results in any arrests and far fewer result in convictions. The victim suffers as much when the crime is unsolved as when the culprit is caught and convicted.

The state should therefore pay compensation to the victims of personal injury by crime. When a victim reports a crime involving personal injury, a part of regular police practice should be to hand him information on a simple procedure of application to a board for compensation. Several states now have such boards. After the state has paid the determined amount it should have the right and duty to recover as much of it as possible from the perpetrator of the injury.

The criminal should be required to pay restitution to the victim or recompensation to the state in all possible cases. The public tax burden will thus be held down. Equally important, as the offender is paying to recompense the victim, whether directly or through the state, he is learning to assume responsibility for his acts.

We have not spoken of compensation for crimes exclusively against property. Where schemes of compensation are in effect in modern, industrialized countries and American states, property crimes are usually excluded. If they were included there would be greatly expanded opportunity for fraudulent claims. Moreover, losses from personal injury are likely to be much harder to bear. When considerable amounts of property are taken by street crime there is usually insurance. Losses to fraud are a serious problem, but difficult to handle when restitution from the criminal cannot be compelled.

In any case, compensation for personal injury is a clear and practical obligation. Public neglect of the victim must be promptly ended.

We should also give more consideration to possible future vic-

tims by planning more carefully to prevent crime. Often someone arises to complain that we have given too much attention
to criminals and not enough to victims of crime. Agreed! But
usually such speeches turn immediately to demand harsher, more
dehumanizing, or even violent treatment of the criminals. Instead of turning our concern to the victims, the speakers only call
for more of the already prevalent concentrated vindictive attention to the criminals which actually aggravates hostilities in widening circles and increases crime.

If we are truly concerned about victims, we will not only see
that they are compensated, but also take new approaches to the
prevention and handling of crime which offer more promise, or
even demonstrated success, in reducing crime. What changes,
then, ought we to make—besides fortifying the community and
compensating victims of crime? The last two chapters will give
some answers.

17. Changes Demanded by the American Conscience

Limiting the Burden of Criminal Law.

The Puritans enacted criminal laws against a remarkably wide
variety of acts. If they thought something was sinful, that was
reason enough to make it a crime. Their list of crimes included
such things as scolding, being absent from church, and making
statements which the ministers said were heretical. The law made
execution the punishment for a teenager's disobedience of his
parents, although it is doubted that the penalty of death was ever
actually imposed for this offense.

The Puritan equating of sin and crime started a trend. Whenever Americans are annoyed by some kind of conduct or feel strongly that some activity is sinful, they are likely to respond, "There ought to be a law . . ." Soon a bill is in the legislative hopper and there may then be another addition to the list of legally defined crimes.

Experience shows that it is impossible to enforce effectively criminal laws against kinds of activities of which there are no unwilling individual victims. The vain effort to enforce such laws unduly burdens the police, the courts and the correctional agencies, uselessly subjects millions of persons to the dehumanizing indignities of criminal proceedings and punishment and lays great costs on the taxpayers without positive results. Such effort also reduces respect for the law and makes it harder to enforce laws which we need for our protection.

Examples of legal futility are criminal laws against public drunkenness, gambling, use of marijuana, and sexual relations between consenting adults.

For *drunkenness* alone two million people are arrested each year—one-third of all arrests made. These arrests are not for drunken driving or assaults, but simply for being drunk in public. Many chronic alcoholics are in court regularly, in the mornings following police arrests and nights of drying out in jail. Some judges fine and release them. Others invariably hand out sentences of 5, 30, 60, or 90 days in jail. Neither fine nor jail cures the alcoholism nor benefits defendant or public in any way. The taxpayer picks up the cost of police arrest procedures, the court, and the support in jail.

Every community should have available an overnight lodging house to which police or, even better, small buses operated by teams of civilians for this purpose, bring drunks found staggering, bewildered, or fallen on the street. Next morning they should be offered treatment, but without coercion, since coercive treatment is a futile waste of money and people. If a drunken person seriously resists his would-be rescuers at pickup, then police should be called and if he resists them with force, appropriate charges should be placed. Such a system is financially less expensive than routine arrest and court action under criminal law. It is also more humane and more effective. Meanwhile, it frees police, courts, and crowded jails for handling serious crime.

Gambling is inconsistently and sporadically dealt with as a crime in most states. In many jurisdictions the more affluent citizens flock to racetracks by the thousands for legal gambling. Off-track bookies and numbers operators in the city do illegal business with poor people and others. Because this business is illegal it feeds the treasuries of organized crime without competition from legal establishments. In no way is gambling prevented by this public policy. Instead, countless citizens, police, and public officials are drawn into cooperation with organized criminal syndicates.

State lotteries are one answer, but their advertising gives an impression of public approval and promotion which gambling does not deserve. A better scheme is the licensing and taxing of public organizations of strong, established purpose, with advertising limited. Of course violation of such administrative control would lead to criminal prosecution.

Many sins are legal. Repealing criminal law against a form of behavior in no way implies ethical approval of it. I regard gambling as immoral and socially destructive. All of us who so believe ought to teach our reasons, not ask the law to do what it plainly cannot do.

Marijuana is much less addictive than alcohol, and also much less productive of criminal acts excepting as its purchase or sale is itself treated as criminal. Other drugs produce varying effects. All the addictive drugs, even including marijuana, are damaging to full human freedom and responsibility. This indictment includes many drugs used under prescription or without prescription by millions of Americans who seek to sleep better, to keep alert after inadequate sleep, or otherwise prop themselves up artificially. The use of most drugs, including marijuana, would better be decriminalized and their sale subjected to controls similar to those now applied to prescription drugs.

Laws against *vagrancy* are highly discriminatory. Rich people are not arrested for being without employment or fixed address. The hazy wording of vagrancy laws makes it possible for the police to arrest almost anyone for whom they harbor personal dislike or vague suspicions.

Disorderly conduct is sometimes highly disruptive and injurious to legitimate interests of merchants, shoppers, or others. But laws against it should be specifically and carefully drawn. Otherwise they are subject to serious police abuse.

The churches and synagogues of America teach that *sexual relations without marriage and in violation of marriage* vows are sinful. I believe that such ethical teaching is important and that the stability of our society is seriously threatened by the increase in premarital and extramarital relations. It is plainly not true that there has always been such a quantity of sex outside of marriage. If you doubt it, then consider this fact. Despite the greatly increased knowledge and convenience of birth control, recorded illegitimate births grew from 3.5% to 10.7% of all live births between 1940 and 1970, doubling between 1960 and 1970 (*Statistical Abstract of the U.S.* 1974, p. 56).

But notice that this has occurred while all sexual intercourse of persons not married partners has been a crime according to the statutes of nearly all states. Such criminal laws should be repealed as unenforceable and as applied only in the most outrageously discriminating way against some powerless people whom the police dislike. It would also be more wholesome if everyone knew that the regulation of sexual conduct of adults was a responsibility of the individual and social conscience, not of legal compulsion.

Every jurisdiction has other laws or ordinances which demean the law by being unenforceable, vague and discriminating or petty.

Reducing Violence and Danger.

Drunken driving kills and injures more persons than all the Index crimes combined. Yet it is not taken very seriously by the criminal laws and procedures of most states. Norway and Sweden have nearly eliminated deaths from drunken driving by rigorous enforcement of criminal laws directed against this menace. The police stop any driver suspected of being under alcoholic influence. He is required to take a breath test then and there.

If he refuses or flunks the test he is arrested and taken to a police station for a blood test. If the proportion of alcohol in his blood exceeds 50 mg per 100 ml (0.05%) his license is forfeited for a year and in court he is almost invariably sentenced to prison for a short term as well—sometimes serving his sentence over weekends until the specified time has accumulated. Several European countries have similar laws, though usually making 80 mg rather than 50 mg the critical figure and mostly somewhat less rigorous and consistent in enforcement—and in results.

It is estimated from special studies that more than half of all deaths from motor vehicle accidents in the United States involve an intoxicated driver. This means that drunken driving kills over 28,000 people per year in this country. If we really care for human life, we will move against this greatest of criminal killers.

Guns in private hands have increased in numbers until now there are probably half as many guns as people in the United States. More than half of those guns are handguns which are designed primarily to shoot people. Most people who buy handguns get them to have ready for the defense of themselves and their homes against attackers, burglars, and robbers. When they are used, however, the target is most often a wife or husband, a son or daughter, or a neighborhood acquaintance. Sixty-five percent of criminal homicides in this country are committed by the use of guns, many more than half of them by handguns. Besides all the homicides, guns are the instruments used in nearly two-thirds of the suicides and in large numbers of accidental deaths.

Handguns ought not to be permitted in private hands. Private citizens should be disarmed in stages. First, manufacture, importation, and sale should be prohibited except for a limited number for professional police and other security forces. Then the government should buy up and destroy all in private hands. After a prescribed period it should be a crime to possess a handgun.

While many police persons must be permitted to carry handguns, their use should be closely limited and the police held strictly accountable for deaths or injuries caused by them. Such accountability should be to joint police-citizen committees, not to police alone.

Rifles and shotguns should be licensed to people meeting specific requirements of sanity, intelligence, and rudimentary training—comparable to requirements for motor vehicle driving licenses. Repeated polls indicate that over 70% of adult Americans believe that licensing should be required for ownership of any gun. Yet, year after year, meaningful gun control bills die in Congress and most legislatures under the intense opposition of the National Rifle Association. Why do Congressmen listen to the NRA and not to the people? Simply because they think most people do not care enough to express their desire for gun control at the ballot box, while the supporters of the NRA will oppose for reelection any Congressman who votes for gun control.

For Equal Justice.

Better paid, better trained *police* are imperatively needed, to do their specialized task well, in service of rich and poor, black and white citizens alike.

We must *eliminate plea bargaining* altogether. As long as it exists, people who have power and money in their hands will drive bargains which make a mockery of the law, while the weak and poor will be betrayed. On this point, the National Advisory Commission on Criminal Justice Standards and Goals agrees—though allowing too long a time for plea bargaining to be phased out. We will return to this subject.

Where *juries* can still be selected in such a way that the class or race of a defendant is not represented at all, a fair trial is usually impossible. Consider, for example, the recent case of a black surgeon convicted by an all-white jury with ten Roman

Catholic members for the death of the fetus in his legal abortion of a black woman. When a poor and ill-educated person is tried before a judge who is usually of the middle or upper class, it is especially important that the defendant have access to a jury including a number of persons drawn from his own class.

To correct the present *gross inequalities of sentences* not reflecting significant differences between convicted individuals, we need some of the changes recommended by Judge Marvin E. Frankel. Review panels of judges should be established to review all sentences and change in either direction those which seem out of line. To make this procedure more effective, every sentencing judge should be required to state concisely the reasons for selecting the actual sentence pronounced within the limits prescribed by the law.

The laws, too, need to be brought into systematic consistency and relevance to the modern scene. As the Advisory Commission recommends, any state which has not overhauled its array of criminal laws within the last ten years should carefully design and adopt a whole *new penal code*. As the legislators do this, they should seek the best knowledge of experience in the control of crime, rather than reacting to the latest waves of emotion in the populace.

If glaring discrimination is not to occur, then all *laws providing for the death penalty must be repealed*. The United States Supreme Court accurately observed that in those states which had been using the death penalty, the individuals executed were only a sample from the much larger number who had committed the same crimes and there was no substantial and proper reason for the discrepancy. We observed earlier that capital punishment, when used, tends rather to increase homicides than to reduce them. The main effects are to discriminate and so increase hostilities and to express the belief that violence is the best solution of our problems. Both of these effects fertilize the seedbeds of crime.

For Swift and Surer Justice.

We have advocated that plea bargaining be abolished. Many judges and other court officials say that is impossible. If the nearly 90% of criminal convictions by guilty pleas were not relieving the courts of the necessity for determining guilt, the delays would be even longer than they are now. Instead, we must shorten drastically the period from arrest to trial and final disposition. The Constitution guarantees to "the accused . . . the right to a speedy and public trial . . ." (Amendment VI). I will suggest soon how this can be accomplished.

Defendants who are out on bail while awaiting trial often seek delays by many devices. Witnesses may die, their memories of events are bound to become less acute and so their testimony becomes more vulnerable to cross-examination. The public's interest in the case is likely to wane and so the defendant and his counsel think he has much to gain by delay. At the same time, the public has much to lose, since the deterrent effect of punishment depends on both its speed and its certainty. On the other hand, the poor defendant who has not the money needed for bail must often stay in jail while awaiting trial. This stay may be for a year or longer and after all this incarceration he may be found innocent. In either case, then, justice is diminished by delay.

How may such delay be avoided, even while we place on the courts the responsibility of convicting by trial and not by plea bargaining? The added task is not quite so great as it first appears. Without plea bargaining many persons charged will plead guilty by their own free choice. As for the rest, there are several means available for lightening the load of the courts. Decriminalizing drunkenness, vagrancy, gambling, use of drugs, and consensual sex between adults will take more than half the criminal case load out of the courts. In civil cases, suits for damages in motor vehicle accidents constitute by far the largest category. Then adopt genuine no-fault motor vehicle insurance! Massachusetts has demonstrated that the public gains lower costs and quicker settlements, while the courts are relieved of one burdensome kind of litigation. Many minor misdemeanors, including petty infraction of motor vehicle laws, now tried in criminal court, should be handled by notices of fines due to be paid in person or by mail at a traffic office and should go to court only if the person charged with the offense asks for public trial.

What else can be done to speed the work of the courts and add to their efficiency? They need a large dose of modern methodical management. Court officials often claim that there is no way to avoid the present uncertain court calendars, frequent postponements and slow movement. They point out that it is not so simple to get opposing attorneys, witnesses, judge, clerk, and necessary documents to the same place at one appointed time. This is true. But management specialists in industry efficiently coordinate much more complex operations every day. Chief Justice Warren E. Burger rightly insists that the courts should cast off their easygoing horse-and-buggy methods and enter the present age of computerized coordination. Besides enabling the courts to get more done and give defendants the promised speedy trial, this would bring in a new day for witnesses now incensed at days lost waiting in court for a particular case to be called.

Diverting Juveniles from Schools of Crime.

Most of the more hardened and difficult inmates of our prisons are graduates of those productive schools of crime, the schools for juvenile delinquents. Take a boy ten, twelve, or fourteen years old, running with an aggressive, reckless gang through a series of scrapes with the law. Find in juvenile court that his home is unfit. Put him in a reform school, industrial school, or whatever the institution may now be called. Label him thus as a young tough, in fact a budding criminal. He begins to swagger and boast of doing worse things than he has done. His biggest embarrassment in the institution is that he has not done anything nearly as bad as the big shots among the older boys. "Next time" he will make up for that.

Many multiple recidivists in our prisons have told me how scared they were when, as young boys, they were first locked up in the special schools. If they had been sent home after a week, they would have vowed never to get in trouble again, they say. But in time a boy is compelled by his human nature to get used to the condition and society in which he finds himself. The one thing most of the boys have in common is their quarrel with parents, schools, and the law. They feed on their common hostility to the establishment. Many of the poorly paid security officers of the institutions stoke up the angry flames by browbeating the boys and abusing them in a wide variety of ways. As the weeks and months pass, a state of chronic warfare with the dominant adult society becomes accepted as the normal, routine condition of life. Either the boy escapes, is put back inside under harder conditions until he escapes again, or he maintains a good appearance the sooner to be released, with the inner hostility still seething. Either route is likely soon to take him into bigger offenses, prepared to go on to our schools of more advanced education in crime—the adult prisons.

How break the cycle? It would be hard enough if we could start now with only first offenders to confront in the juvenile court. Actually, the police, the judge, and the probation officers must face, in the majority of young offenders, boys and increasingly girls too, who have already been hardened in lawless patterns by previous sentences. Can their line of development be broken now so that they can be turned in a new direction?

Jerome G. Miller is convinced that there are promising alternatives to juvenile schools of crime, even for most boys already hardened in antisocial patterns. Before 1969, Massachusetts had five residential institutions for juvenile delinquents, much like such schools in other states. In 1969, Miller, as commissioner of youth services, began gradual efforts to change them and phase them out of existence. The vested interests of staff members, local merchants, and others, as well as fear of change and bureaucratic inertia, frustrated his efforts. In a kind of desperation, after making dramatic appearances on television and cultivating as much political support as possible, he abruptly closed all those institutions, moving the youthful residents elsewhere. After Miller left to assume analogous duties in Illinois, his successor, Howard Leavy pursued similar policies. Where are the delinquent Massachusetts boys now?

In December 1974, Massachusetts had a total of 2,030 boys and girls under active care of the Department of Youth Services. Of the total, 41% (835) were on traditional probation or parole in their own homes. Of the remaining 1,195 juveniles, 51% were in their own homes with special aid and supervision provided for them and their families, in boarding schools with children not in trouble, in the homes of relatives or in new wholesome ventures of special, individually adapted character. Twenty-eight percent (334) were in group homes for which the state had signed contracts. About 15% were in foster care homes. Only 9% (113) were in secure and intensive care.

While it is too early to boast of long-term results, the facts collected in the first careful, independent research on the boys are promising. The rate of recidivism within six months of release was less than half what it was under the old program. The boys' own reports of their attitudes and relations with the community were dramatically improved over similar reports by boys in the old regime responding to the same questions. How many boys "run"—that is escape from supervision? About the same proportion run now from unlocked houses as ran from the most tightly locked and controlled of the old institutions! Meaningful programs and concerned people now hold them as well as locks, bolts, and guards could do formerly.

Experiments with selected parts of the delinquent juvenile populations in other states also look promising. If so much hope can be raised in dealing with boys who include many with values already twisted by previous incarcerations, how much better results can we obtain when few or none of such graduates of our old schools of crime are longer in the juvenile populations!

Alternatives to Present Prisons.

Some criminal offenders are so dangerous that they must be locked up for a time. But correctional officers generally agree that this is true of only a small fraction of people now held in our prisons and jails. The one punishment of imprisonment has become our routine method of dealing with convicted criminals. We call the system "corrections," but as we observed earlier, little happens in most prisons and almost nothing in jails which corrects the conduct of anyone. Much happens which embitters, dehumanizes and brutalizes people. Experience shows that as they are now operated, prisons on the whole increase the criminal tendencies of their inmates besides exacting a frightful toll of human and economic waste (as described in Chapter 5). What alternatives are there? Here are some recommendations.

1. Sharply reduce jailing before trial. According to law, every person arrested is presumed innocent until proved guilty. Many such persons are in fact innocent. Yet on any given day there are hundreds of thousands of such persons in American jails awaiting trial. People of means usually get out on bond which many of the poor cannot afford.

The Vera institute, working with the courts in New York, has selected large proportions of defendants who would ordinarily be detained for trial or released only on bail and has released them on their own recognizance or under personal supervision of responsible citizens. This experiment has not resulted in more crimes by persons awaiting trial and the Vera-released defendants have a better record of appearance for trial than defendants on bail.

Such release of selected defendants must be spread and multiplied throughout the country. Meanwhile, as we have already urged, criminal trials must be speeded up. If an arrested person is tried quickly, then the person who appears to be such a poor risk that he cannot be released will be held for only a very short time before acquittal or sentence. These two procedures together with our proposals for taking off the statute books the totally ineffective laws against drunkenness and the like, would reduce our *jail* population to a minor fraction of the present level.

2. In sentencing, incarcerate only as a last resort. The 1972 Penal Code of the State of Hawaii makes precisely this requirement and even specifies many circumstances which every judge should see as indications that a particular convicted offender must *not* be incarcerated. Imprisonment is so likely to increase alienation, hostility, and despair—all conditions tending to increase crime—that its use ought to be sharply reduced on that ground. In addition, the sheer human waste and suffering which it now causes, with no positive good to anyone, are imperative reasons for reducing it drastically.

3. Reduce the number of long sentences. When people must be imprisoned, sentences should usually be much shorter than now. We must stress again that sentences served in the United States, crime for crime, are the longest in any developed Western country. The waste caused by this policy is a national horror and disgrace.

4. Use fines scaled to ability to pay and to the profits of crime. A fine of $1,000 for a rich man is a light tap on the wrist; for

a man who has just made a million dollars by dishonest stock transactions it is ludicrous. For a poor man it is likely to be impossible. In some cases arrangements should be made for paying by installments withheld from wages or other income.

5. Require restitution by the offender to the victim(s), as recommended in the preceding chapter. This should serve as a partial or total alternative to imprisonment.

6. Use work-release and part-time incarceration when appropriate. Programs of releasing prisoners for daytime work on farms, in industries, and elsewhere in the community are now widely used with good results, not only with misdemeanants but also with serious youthful offenders and adult felons. After faithfully returning from work to the prison daily for a time, the inmate is often granted occasional weekend home furloughs, with generally good results. In various foreign countries, convicted misdemeanants are frequently given permission to serve their entire short sentences in weekends or weekends and evenings. The National Advisory Commission recommends large uses of such arrangements in this country.

Social Restoration After Crime.

Probably a large majority of persons being released from prison are determined not to get into further trouble with the law. Often it seems as if all the forces of society join to compel them to break such commitments and plunge them more deeply into crime. Decent citizens avoid their company. Employers refuse them jobs. Housing is hard for them to find. They know that they could still get money by burglary, robbery, the drug traffic, or other illegal activities. Racketeers may recognize them and offer them opportunities in crime. "Don't be a sap," they say. "Nobody wants you. Ya gonna starve? I'll take care of you." The road to crime seems the only road open.

If the individual is to become a law-abiding citizen, he must be offered restoration of full rights to employment in keeping with his skill and intelligence, even if not always the same work in which he has betrayed his trust earlier. We need to restore him to equal opportunity for housing, for participation in sports, church life, and whatever else may signal private and public acceptance.

More than that, the social rift from which the crime came and which it has extended or deepened needs to be addressed. Substandard housing needs to be upgraded, unemployment must be reduced to the vanishing point. Millions of persons are eager to contribute to the services and production needed by millions and they want to be decently supported by their own labor, yet are refused the opportunity. This is intolerable. All hands are needed and if private industry cannot employ them, then the public must for the public and private good. Slogans of "private enterprise" or "the American way" are a poor substitute for food, health care, housing, and opportunity to play a meaningful part in the work of the community.

A part of this social restoration is also the turning from the false goals of America B, with its selfish destructiveness and crime-producing alienations. The public overcoming of unemployment and desperate poverty is itself both a test and a means of cultivating America A, which alone offers hope for our society and the world. The two go together—the outward action of solving problems cooperatively and the inner commitment of will to place the public good above private advantage.

18. Volunteers Needed

Crime, together with the ills which nurture it and the similar evils which it produces, is every citizen's business. If we leave it to the professionals—police, prosecutors, judges, correctional officials, and trained therapists—crime will continue to spread and worsen. It is too big for the specialized groups to handle. Besides, both the causes and consequences of crime reach far outside the scope of the criminal justice system. There are so many ways in which volunteers can help that it is impossible even to list them all, let alone write an account of each here. All we can do is to present some important samples and hope the reader's imagination and concern will go on from there to find his or her own opportunity for service.

The National Advisory Commission on Criminal Justice Standards and Goals estimates that two and one-half million volunteers are at work in relation to various phases of the criminal justice system. Although the Commission asks for many more, the

figure quoted may give an inflated impression. Many volunteers have only a marginal or indirect relation or serve only rarely. On the other hand, I have met many who are truly impressive in their sacrificial devotion to their chosen tasks. The need is for several million others.

Aid to Victims.

Whether public funds or payments by offenders or neither provide compensation, voluntary aid to victims of crime is needed. Women and girls who have been forcibly raped often need thoughtful counsel and sympathetic support, as well as medical assistance. A network of centers for aid to rape victims is now at work in many large cities and some small ones. Usually volunteers in such centers cooperate with physicians and attorneys, often with professional counselors as well.

Large numbers of other victims need friends to help them recover confidence and to provide material aid in their rehabilitation, especially if they have been left with physical handicaps. Americans have often given heart-warming response to appeals for aid to victims of fire, storm, flood, or earthquake. But crimes turn most people's attention exclusively to the offender. The parable of the good Samaritan who cared for a man robbed and wounded on the Jericho Road has touched the hearts of most Christians and many non-Christians as well. We need to put it into more widespread literal practice.

Care for Offenders and Their Families.

The family of a man or woman sentenced to prison often suffers financial hardship, humiliation, grief, and strained relations with neighbors. Volunteers help to establish and maintain communication with the person behind bars, to apply for needed public assistance, to maintain self-respect and to gain friendly reinforcement. Such aid may protect the family from permanent disruption and prevent additional members from running afoul of the law. Many organizations which supply voluntary assistance to inmates of correctional institutions try to find ways of helping families as well. Whether a volunteer begins with the inmate or family, his service is usually most effective when it can include both.

Will the offender commit new crimes when he is released? Or will he go straight and help to guide others into law-abiding and useful lives? Often the answer depends on the availability of a volunteer to befriend him in jail or prison, to find out what is disturbing him, to help him form new positive goals, and then to be there outside to assist him in attaining them.

A volunteer has two big advantages over a professional therapist, counselor, or parole officer. The inmate is likely to be a little skeptical about either one at first meeting. But the volunteer who is genuine finds it much easier to overcome the initial suspicion and convince the inmate that he is personally concerned for his well-being. Even more important is the fact that the volunteer can relate to one person or a small group, while the official nearly always has responsibility for many. A parole officer may be obliged to look after 100 or more people. The greater part of his time will be inevitably devoted to making records and reports. How personal would you expect his relations with individuals under his supervision to be?

The National Advisory Commission, in its 1973 report on *Community Crime Prevention* (p. 15) illustrates the effectiveness which may be achieved by a voluntary program. The report refers to the Volunteers in Probation led by Judge Keith Leenhouts of Royal Oak, Michigan. Says the commission, "When probationers from Royal Oak were compared with probationers from nonvolunteer courts, it was found that not only were those from Royal

Oak less hostile, but their recidivism rates were drastically lower
—15 percent compared with nearly 50 percent." The report
adds that the "Board of Christian Social Concerns of the Metho-
dist Church . . . provided funds to spread the idea throughout the
country. . . . Since 1969, the idea has spread to approximately
2,090 courts, prisons and juvenile institutions" (p. 305).

Offender Aid and Restoration U.S.A. works in city and county
jails of Virginia, North Carolina, Maryland, and New York, while
facing requests for help in starting new work in several other
states. OAR establishes relationships of confidence with correctional officials, as it recruits and trains volunteers. Besides working
on a one-to-one basis with jail inmates, OAR encourages the
development of alternatives to incarceration both before and
after sentencing.

Many local churches and councils of churches perform a wide
variety of voluntary services. They include providing tutors and
reading material, establishing rooms for the lodging of parolees
and releasees just coming out of jail or prison, securing employment and helping establish wholesome social relationships in the
community. The Chamber of Commerce of the United States is
nationally publicizing needs for changes in corrections and is
campaigning for businessmen to employ ex-offenders.

Other volunteers sponsor and advise self-help organizations
inside prisons, such as prison chapters of Alcoholics Anonymous,
Seventh Step and the Junior Chamber of Commerce. Some provide
foster homes or group homes for juvenile delinquents, usually with
public subsidies to cover part or all of the cost. At West Virginia
Wesleyan College, two seniors and a graduate of the preceding
year financed and established the New Dawn Youth Center where
judges of two counties send selected juvenile delinquents. The
enthusiasm and realistic strength of the young proprietors, with
their faculty advisor John Warner, have won remarkable support
from the community. The process of eliciting this support has

set in motion forces which will carry far beyond the few boys and girls cared for at the center.

You may be able to learn of volunteer programs near home, relating to your particular interest and capacity, by inquiring of local probation or prison officials or a local church office. One office maintains information on all kinds of voluntary organizations throughout the country concerned with victims, courts, corrections, diversionary programs and reentry. That office is happy to provide relevant information to any concerned inquirer and also to sell a variety of training materials. It is the National Information Center on Volunteerism, Dr. Ivan Scheier, Director, P.O. Box 4179, Boulder, Colorado 80302.

Assisting the Police.

Most police action occurs in response to calls from citizens. As noted in the first chapter, only about half the serious crimes are reported to the police. Even of those reported many must be dropped because no witnesses will testify. Most people feel reluctant to report having witnessed a crime. Unless we overcome this reluctance we have no right to complain that the law is not enforced.

Some citizens usefully volunteer to act as marshals for protest parades or to form auxiliary forces available to augment the regular police at times of special stress or in areas of high crime rates. The police of New York City have "recruited 14,000 unarmed 'block watchers'—civilian volunteers who are trained in techniques of observing and reporting crime. The city has also organized 6,000 taxi drivers and a corps of private motorists to report suspicious occurrences on the streets and highways" (*Newsweek*, September 16, 1974, p. 53).

The National Advisory Commission reports with implied approval other volunteer programs in which citizens assist in law enforcement in Sacramento, Buffalo, Kalamazoo, Joliet, Battle Creek, St. Paul, Kansas City (Missouri), Boston, other cities, and several counties. The volunteers help staff police offices, distribute information, watch for suspicious evidences of possible criminal behavior and report to headquarters, or patrol stores to watch for shoplifters.

The more citizens are involved in all these nonviolent actions to assist law enforcement, the more the power of public opinion is brought to bear, both on potential lawbreakers and on the system. In this way many incipient criminal careers are ended early and there will be less resort to force and confinement.

Diversionary Programs.

Volunteers in many cities keep certain telephones staffed twenty-four hours a day and advertise that they will welcome calls from anyone inclined to suicide or feeling depressed or simply needing a friendly ear. These telephones are much used. Many people report that such calls have saved them from desperate acts of various kinds.

Several churchmen in England led by John Dodd and supported by churches and individual benefactors established and operate the Langley House (now actually eleven houses). This is called "a Christian venture in the after care of homeless offenders." Without the Langley House, most of the men would either be remaining in prison for want of any other place to go or would be wanderers, probably soon getting into trouble and returning to prison. The 200 men in the houses range in age from seventeen to old age and in numbers from 8 to 23 per house. Each house is managed by a resident couple, usually with children. About half of the men being sheltered go out to work daily, some of the younger ones are in school and many work around the place, on attached farms or in a home industry. Some have never before in their lives experienced a home where a man and wife lived together with their children. Individuals who cannot make it on their own may remain permanently. Others, more confident after the security of being accepted in a well-ordered home, move out into quarters of their own, with or without marrying. Often they come back to visit for counsel and reassurance.

Teen Challenge, an American organization now working also abroad, operates with many volunteers along with paid staff members. This organization has a strong motivation arising from conservative Protestant convictions. It specializes in the care of drug addicts the majority of whom come from courts or prisons. However, Teen Challenge also takes in many boys and some men who have never been arrested but are addicted and are diverted from the criminal justice system only by turning to Teen Challenge in time.

Of course innumerable friendly neighbors, teachers, and staff members at school, ministers, recreational directors, and others intervene at signs of trouble and turn boys or girls away from delinquency and crime. Efforts in crisis intervention and diversion are bounded only by the limits of concern and creative resourcefulness of interested people.

Work with Courts.

The National Advisory Commission reports an estimate that in all "some 100,000 volunteers" are "affiliated with well over 1,000 courts" (*Community Crime Prevention,* p. 15). Most courts in the larger cities and some elsewhere are understaffed to carry the workload and this is one cause of their running behind, with consequent delays. Volunteers render a variety of services, such as typing or carrying messages. Many other volunteers are at the call of judges to take a friendly interest in juveniles or adults whom the judges are reluctant to incarcerate or even to put on formal probation, but who do appear to need a steadying, wise friend to provide special guidance and help.

A different kind of input is made in communities where citizen groups institute a court watch. Visits are scheduled so that one or two are present and taking notes (unless that is forbidden) at all times when criminal proceedings are in progress. They let the judge know, in a friendly way, that they are doing this because they are concerned as citizens to know how criminal cases are being handled in their community and to see if they can be helpful in making the criminal justice system serve the whole community better. Such watching not only educates the members of the organization doing the observing, but establishes the kind of relationships likely to produce more responsible and equitable sentencing. It also provides leverage for efforts to make changes.

Changing the System.

You and other informed and concerned citizens hold the only keys to changing the present ineffective, unjust, and destructive system for handling crime. Legislatures and Congress respond to pressures from citizen groups. The rank and file of people with jobs in the present system generally oppose change. Every change of system is feared because of a possible threat to their employment. In corrections many officers fear also that changes might make their work more dangerous. Actually, many changes can decrease the perils now attending work in the prisons. But when tensions are high and nerves taut present risks are likely to be less frightening than new ones. Besides, there is a great inherent inertia in every large bureaucracy. There is even more of such inertia in the prison bureaus than in most others.

What constituency, then, will demand change? The prison inmates feel most personally and painfully the need for change. But most of them have always been poor, with limited education and little influence. Whatever was the previous state of a person convicted of crime, the conviction has discredited him. Most citizens do want to see something done about crime, but most demands are emotional and uninformed. The result of citizen outcries about crime is likely to be bigger police forces, added police hardware, bigger prisons and more severe sentences for the small proportion of offenders caught and convicted. In other words, there is usually a continuance of the same ineffective, self-defeating system, only more of it.

We desperately need better policies for preventing crime and more just and effective ways of dealing with it when it occurs. If we are to have them, citizens without special interests must become informed, organize and lobby urgently and persistently. In this task, one important resource is the 1973 report of the National Advisory Commission on Criminal Justice Standards and Goals. The stated Standards and Goals will have only so much effect as concerned citizens make them have. The new commitments of the United States Chamber of Commerce are encouraging and their free literature is useful. The American Bar Association reports and office are helpful on a number of the needed changes. The National Council on Crime and Delinquency is an especially fruitful source of information and ideas. For some projects the Law Enforcement Assistance Administration will provide funds.

You will probably not find the proposals you wish to support backed by all the above organizations and agencies, while other interests will strongly oppose change. Concerned citizens need to join coalitions to support particular aims they hold in common, and other coalitions for pursuit of other goals, while seeking to broaden the objectives of all.

In most communities the best first step is group study. After studying together some of the related pamphlets, magazine articles, and books, the group should gather firsthand information. Arrange to visit criminal courts, jails, prisons, and juvenile institutions on a systematic basis. Compare observations with the

Standards and Goals and with your own beliefs about true justice. Then move into action, gathering allies and learning more as you go.

Gaining access to the correctional institutions may not be easy. Church groups may arrange to assist chaplains with music, religious education of inmates, or counseling. Individuals may join or organize new chapters of volunteer associations. Sometimes a direct offer of help to a superintendent, warden, or sheriff will open doors of opportunity. Patience and persistence may be required. Officials of correctional institutions are usually short-staffed, anxious about security, and wanting to avoid any new complications of their hard tasks.

All citizens have responsibility for developing the kind of community they should have. Few things are such clear signs of moral and social sickness as crime. Few things affect the health of the community so much as its methods for coping with crime. Criminal justice is everybody's business.

Promoting America A.

We have seen sufficient crime in high places recently to show that economic means and political power alone are not enough to keep people out of crime. In fact the power of wealth and political office are themselves temptations to crime.

Extreme imbalance of wealth, power, and opportunity is productive of crime. It tempts people near the top to illegal abuses of power. The political fathers of our republic knew this and their awareness of it was precisely the reason why they introduced our constitutional system of checks and balances in government. We have seen recently how dependent we are on the watchfulness of Congress and the courts to check crime in the executive branch before it passes a point of no return in destruction of our liberties.

Meanwhile, extreme poverty and exclusion of some groups from full opportunity to participate in our political and social institutions give rise to the hostility and alienation which spawn street crimes. Even all through middle America there is a disturbing amount of dishonesty, dependence on alcohol and drugs, and neglect or abuse of children in a frantic search for individual pleasure and advantage.

The grave crisis of crime and the irrational, unjust system we have for dealing with it are both deeply rooted in the moral crisis of our culture. If we continue to idealize the tough, aggressive male, rugged and selfish individualism, and the quick resort to violent solutions of our problems, while self-righteously blaming others for our social ills, the American future is dim. America B, in this day of urban crowding, limited resources, extremes of wealth and poverty, and alienating divisions, is the way to ruin.

There is a better American tradition which offers hope. This is America A, the benevolent way of neighborly helpfulness, community responsibility, simplicity of life, and gentle reasonableness. Whoever enlarges the scope of these attitudes and habits in action is striking at the root of crime. People do this when they promote the more inclusive ways of economic sharing which are so desperately needed to eliminate the widening gap between rich and poor. When we care for victims, offenders, and the families of both, we are helping restore them to full community and also helping ourselves to participate more completely in America A. When we persuade other people to join our efforts, we further expand the fortification of the community against crime.

In such ways as these we build America the beautiful and the future which our better conscience and higher hopes demand.

QUESTIONS FOR THOUGHT

1. What do you think needs to be done to extend opportunity for full participation in American economic, social, and political life to classes of people now excluded in practice?

2. Should your community be doing more to provide opportunities for employment and recreation for youth?

3. Is there a problem of corruption in your local community? What should be done about corruption at the various levels where it exists?

4. Have you, a member of your family, or a friend been the victim of a serious crime, either against the person or against property? Did the criminal law and procedure give any assistance? Were the procedures a further burden? Did the community help?

5. Do you agree that victims of crime ought to be compensated for personal injuries received? By whom? How should this be arranged?

6. What are the laws of your town, county, and state concerning public drunkenness? Are they helpful? What changes in law or facilities would you support?

7. Are changes needed in the laws concerning gambling which are in effect in your area? Do the laws apply equally to all classes?

8. Do the churches and schools of your community effectively teach for responsible marriage? Are sexual acts of consenting adults outside marriage legally defined as crimes? Are the laws helpful?

9. Do the laws under which you live distinguish between marijuana and the opiate or hallucinogenic drugs? Do you think they should? Are the laws easier on alcohol than

on marijuana? Are there sound reasons for the provisions of such laws?

10. How is drunken driving handled in your state? Would you support the legal provision urged in Chapter 17?

11. Can criminal justice be made truly just and crime reduced to low levels without sharply narrowing the gap between the richest and poorest in our society? Can a defensible community adequately bridge this gap without reducing it? How would you deal with this problem?

12. How can you best help as a volunteer to meet needs outlined in the last chapter? Will you?

Suggested Further Reading

L. Harold DeWolf, *Crime and Justice in America: A Paradox of Conscience*. New York: Harper & Row, 1975.

Stephen Schafer, *The Victim and His Criminal*. Paperback. New York: Random House, 1968.

National Advisory Commission on Criminal Justice Standards and Goals. Report (5 vols., paperback). Washington, D.C.: U.S. Government Printing Office, 1973. Also available in one-volume paperback summary volume.